The traits of today's CFO

A handbook for excelling in an evolving role

Ron Rael, CPA

CGMA

Chartered Global Management Accountant®

Powered by

Notice to Readers

The Traits of Today's CFO: A Handbook for Excelling in an Evolving Role does not represent an official position of the American Institute of Certified Public Accountants, and it is distributed with the understanding that the author and the publisher are not rendering legal, accounting, or other professional services in this publication. If legal advice or other expert assistance is required, the services of a competent professional should be sought.

1 2 3 4 5 6 7 8 9 0 PIP 1 9 8 7 6 5 4 3

ISBN: 978-1-93735-223-3

CONTENTS

INTRODUCTION

You are the conscience of your organisation. Unleash your power.

If you want to be secure in your position as the leader who serves as your organisation's conscience, you must be able to document your worth to your organisation's leaders. At the same time, you are the head of a customer service team whose purpose is to provide superior service to your customers. This is a difficult and challenging position to be in.

This book explores the 10 critical skills that will help you add value to your organisation and boost your career so you quickly move to the next level of accomplishment.

After reading this book, you should be able to

- be the leader that your organisation needs you to be.

- use coaching to make your organisation stronger and better.

- become an advocate and coach for your team.

- develop into a powerful agent for positive change.

- take the 6½ key steps that make you invaluable.

- design a tailored action plan for your specific needs.

Exercise: Are You Replacing Yourself?

Instructions

To complete this self-assessment, place a checkmark next to the questions that you answer with a definite "Yes." Compare the total number of boxes you checked with the answer key at the end.

_____   Are you excited and enthusiastic about going to work each day?

_____   Do you use a wide variety of your skills and talents each day?

_____   Have you made several big mistakes within the last year?

_____   Have you changed what you do as a result of these mistakes?

_____   Are you valued for the interpretation of the information that you provide, in addition to the content of the report itself?

Continued on p. 2

_____ Could your finance team "get the job done" if you were out of commission for more than 45 days?

_____ Have you transformed your team from "doing management accounting" to operating a business unit?

_____ Have you created multiple growth opportunities for each of your direct reports within the last year?

Answer Key

7–8 checked—Congratulations!

You are a leading edge and committed leader. Keep working on building a team that supports your efforts so that you can quickly take on more responsibility.

4–6 checked—You are getting there.

You are not replacing yourself, but you do have your team's priorities in place. Look at the areas where you did not answer "Yes" and get working on these immediately.

0–4 checked—It is not too late.

You must step up to be more of a catalyst for change and manager of people resources. Your insight and talents are needed, but you are not using them. You cannot be timid or complacent because you will soon find yourself overlooked or replaced.

ADVANCED CRITICAL SKILLS

Every CFO and controller needs 10 specific skills to be successful:

1. Thought articulation

2. Crystal clear communication

3. Coaching

4. Honest self-assessing

5. Objective thinking

6. Critical thinking

7. Synthesising

8. Team building

9. Long-term visioning

10. Stepping beyond your comfort zone

When you are able to apply these 10 skills daily for the organisation that employs you, you will find that you have more power and influence than you ever thought possible. You will quickly become more comfortable in your role as the financial leader. The business world demands that the controller, CFO or director of finance be the ultimate authority on what is ethical and beneficial for all the stakeholders of the company. Without confidence, assertiveness, accountability and, most important, commitment, you will be unable to fulfil this role. Therefore, the purpose of this book is to move you beyond your comfort zone and into the role of your organisation's conscience.

This book covers the 18 best practices provided in the following checklist. Check off those that could benefit you or your organisation. Note them on this page as a reminder to go back and explore the practice.

SPECIFIC BEST PRACTICES

- ☐ The Position Description
- ☐ Shape the Culture by Defining It
- ☐ Create Balanced Risk-Taking With a Risk Programme
- ☐ Foster Accountability by Defining It
- ☐ Establish a Governance Programme That Weeds Out Questionable Practices
- ☐ Shape Your Employees' Teaming Behaviours With a Solid Structure
- ☐ Shape Your Employees' Accountability by Establishing Behaviour Expectations
- ☐ Shape Your Employees' Behaviour by Using Honest Feedback
- ☐ Shape Your Employees' Behaviour With Recognition and Rewards
- ☐ Skills Gap Assessment
- ☐ Using a Gap Analysis
- ☐ Formalised Action Plans
- ☐ Action Plan Reporting and Accountability
- ☐ Solution Creator
- ☐ Probing Questions
- ☐ Problem Restatement
- ☐ Instilling a Personal Commitment
- ☐ Instilling Continuous Improvement With Plus-Delta

Exercise: Apply Your Learning

Write out one key lesson that you have acquired during your years of experience as a leader in management accounting.

_____

_____

_____

_____

_____

Continued on p. 4

Explain why this lesson has stayed with you.

_____

_____

_____

_____

_____

Explain how this lesson relates to your view of the role that the controller or CFO plays or should play in an organisation that values integrity and ethical behaviours.

_____

_____

_____

_____

_____

1

STEP 1: IMPROVE YOUR LEADERSHIP EFFECTIVENESS BY LOOKING AHEAD

The pain of change comes from within—your need to face your own ego and self-imposed limitations.

Leaders in management accounting are often so focused on to-do lists, tasks and deadlines that they forget to take time to look at the big picture. This first step is designed to provide a global view of where the role of the CFO and, by extension, the controller is heading. You will quickly discover that the roles they play must change or they will be left behind. In this global economy, speed, flexibility and innovation are paramount.

After reading this chapter you should be able to

- redefine the role we must play to benefit our employers.
- see our evolving profession through recent survey and research results.
- isolate the critical skills that we will need to be effective in the future.
- isolate core attitudes that will benefit us in the future.
- identify the most important changes in management accounting that we address now.

OUR FUTURE—MORE OF THE SAME, AT WARP SPEED

The various components of management accountants' jobs are changing faster than you might imagine.

CFO and Controller's Future Roles

Our primary roles in the next few years, and probably beyond, are as follows.

Collaborator
You must be able to collaborate with everyone in the organisation. You will not be invited to the table and trusted unless you know how to collaborate effectively.

Consultant
Operational managers and executives look to you and your team to offer suggestions for improvement. You must be proactive and consistent in this role.

Communicator

In our near future, communicating takes on a whole new dimension. You and your team must be the truth tellers for the organisation. The data and metrics you report on must be meaningful for everyone.

Strategic Leader

The CFO or controller must be the one taking the initiative to lead strategically.

Fulfiller of the Eight Expectations

Figure 1-1 uses a wheel to represent your team's success. Without a strong, flexible and talented team, you will not be the strategic leader that you must be. Each segment of the wheel represents the expectations and demands placed upon the CFO's team by the CEO, board, managers and other stakeholders.

Figure 1-1: The Eight Expectations of Management Accounting

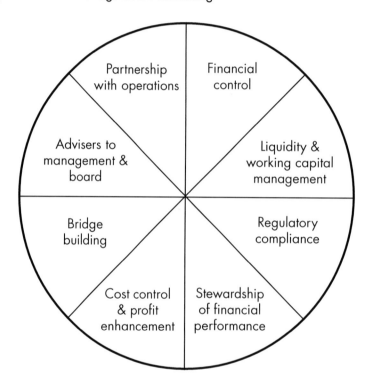

The CFO and Controller Team's Responsibilities

The wheel represents what management accounting must continuously and effectively do.

Assert Financial Control

One responsibility that has not changed for us is ensuring that our organisations have a control system in place that works. Whether you are subject to government regulations, worried about your company's survival, or working for a successful organisation, this role continues to grow in importance.

If you do not take this responsibility seriously, no one else will.

Manage Liquidity and Working Capital

A second responsibility that remains the same is ensuring that your organisation has the funds to operate. This also has grown in importance because of the recent recession's after-effects.

Ensure Regulatory Compliance

Management accountants continue to have the significant responsibility of ensuring that they keep executives and themselves out of prison. Every year there are more rules they must spend time understanding, so that they can help their employer remain compliant.

Be the Stewards of Financial Performance

This stewardship responsibility goes beyond issuing regular reports. The CFO and controller are depended upon to ensure that they are measuring and monitoring all the important success factors of the business and reporting on them. In addition, because their reports will now contain more nonfinancial metrics, they must work to determine the quality of those data points that they do not control.

Carry Out Cost Control and Perform Profit Enhancement

Because staying competitive has become of extreme importance in the global economy, the controller and CFO are expected to offer multiple suggestions on reducing the cost of doing business and enhancing the bottom line. Everyone else in the organisation is narrowly focused on their responsibilities; therefore, the controller and CFO must be focused on the broad strategic picture.

Be Bridge Builders

The management accounting staff can no longer afford to be a silo or an island unto itself. An increasingly important role for us is building bridges with other parts of the organisation, a function that works in parallel with communication.

Be Advisers to Management and the Board

CFOs, controllers and other management accountants in leadership roles are now viewed as key people to whom management and the board turn for advice. If your executives do not include your thoughts in their future planning, then you have not taken on this responsibility.

Partner with Operational Managers

Another responsibility of management accountants is equal partnership with other groups in the organisation, especially operational managers.

The Management Accounting Department's Journey Into the Future

Here is what the future holds for all of us who work in the internal finance function of an organisation: public, private, government, nonprofit and so forth.

We are all in the midst of a major transformation.

If we do not take advantage of this transformation, or even notice that it is occurring, we will continue to be minimised, downsized, chastised, criticised, ostracised or, worse yet, outsourced.

This transformation that the finance team, group or department must make is designed to help our employer stay viable and successful. Making this transition will ensure that we will be seen as a core function.

We must move from being the people who keep the data to the people who keep the trust. This transformation is referred to as a *value creation approach to management accounting*.

VALUE CREATION APPROACH TO MANAGEMENT ACCOUNTING: EIGHT INSIGHTS INTO MANAGEMENT ACCOUNTING'S FUTURE

In the following section are eight different points of view about what the future holds. Each study states similar findings in different ways. As you read each one, look for common or universal themes.

The first theme is the most obvious.

Universal Theme No. 1: An Emphasis on Nonaccounting Roles

Our roles are rapidly expanding far beyond traditional management accounting. This expansion is not a suggestion or a request; it is a mandate.

View 1—Future Perfect: The CFO of Tomorrow

There will always be a high demand for the strategic CFO.

Strategic Transformation

The purpose of this research project was to determine how the role of the management accounting team is changing with all the pressures bombarding it. A key finding was that all the executives surveyed expect a continued transformation of the management accounting group that they employ.

Too Much Transacting

The CFO spends less time today on traditional tasks, yet such work still amounts to about 50% of his or her time. This time-intensive work must be reduced to about 25% of the CFO's day so he or she can spend more time on decision support. Executives said they desire a strategic CFO to be on their team.

Surveyed CFOs said few finance departments have the depth of talent and experience necessary to undertake a more strategic role and assume nonfinancial functions. Making this transition of mindsets and attitudes along with the acquisition of the right skills is a long-term process, so the organisation's senior leaders and CFO must be patient.

You, a Strategic CFO

Three essential areas in which executives want their CFO to improve are the following:

- Stronger and more strategic leadership

- Management

- Communications

The report identified necessary and specific skills that enable the CFO to become an active partner in the business. A leader of finance must perform the following skills extremely well:

- Strategy development
- High-level decision making
- Planning analysis
- High-level negotiating
- Being assertive and outspoken
- Building a collaborative environment
- Being a trusted adviser
- Championing company-wide initiatives

> The CFO of tomorrow should be a big-picture thinker rather than detail-oriented, outspoken rather than reserved, prefer to delegate rather than be hands-on, emphasise what gets done rather than how things get done, and make collaborative rather than unilateral decisions. He or she should also master the ability to foresee the future consequences of current actions, follow through on decisions, and manage projects effectively.

The preceding quote and views expressed in this section are drawn from a report by CFO Research Services in collaboration with KPMG, July 2008.

View 2—The CFO's Role in Achieving Operational Excellence

The role of the CFO is to foster and support organisational excellence.

Excellence Defined

The study's purpose was to determine how much the CFO is involved in operational excellence initiatives. A majority of CFOs said they are already involved, and many said they must become more so. *Operational excellence* is defined as "execution as measured in terms of greater process consistency, lower error rates, higher quality, lower costs, and other metrics that a company considers key to its operating performance."

Your Expanded Role

The CFO's role has expanded from traditional oversight to that of a performance manager, and our new mission is to forge relationships with operational managers so management accounting can provide them with the data that they need, not what the CFOs push on them. CFOs are embracing the important role that finance must take on to help their employer achieve operational excellence. A majority stated that operational knowledge has a substantial impact on their ability to do their jobs. The CFOs expressed the desire to be more involved in improving their employer's operational excellence because they are not content with the status quo.

The definition of excellence for the finance team is to have the ability to add value. The team's ability to do this is dependent on the following four factors:

1. Targeting data and helping managers see the financial impact of decisions
2. Having good communication and leadership skills
3. Fostering a supportive work environment in terms of culture and the executive's priorities
4. Understanding how the business actually operates

To meet this goal, the finance team must enhance its skills in the following areas to improve its involvement and results:

- Interpersonal and communication skills
- Leadership skills
- Operational business experience and knowledge

The CFO's Current Barriers

What stops the CFO from being better at operational excellence?

According to the CFOs responding, operational excellence is affected by

- the amount of support they formally and informally receive from their employer,
- the corporate culture,
- the priorities established by their executives, and
- the type of company for which they work.

Self-Fulfilling Loop

Communication and involvement with operations is a mutually reinforcing loop, as shown in figure 1-2. Greater involvement and communications is a win-win for management accounting.

Figure 1-2: The Finance Manager's Self-Fulfilling Prophecy

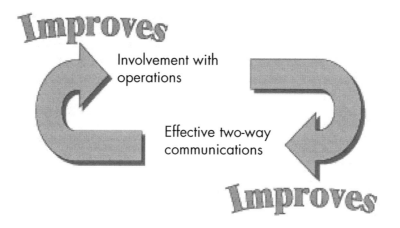

The views expressed in the previous section are drawn from a research project by CFO Research Services in collaboration with Accenture, April 2009.

View 3—Finance's Talent Challenge: How Leading CFOs Are Taking Charge

Restoring Credibility

Because of the damage done by Andrew Fastow and the failure of Enron, the Economist Intelligence Unit wanted to uncover what CFOs are doing to rebuild their credibility and reestablish trust. After surveying 636 executives (9 industry segments, located in 73 different countries), it reported that "the results present a vivid picture of the uphill battle many CFOs face to populate their finance organisations with high-potential individuals who can support and partner with them and the business at large, to help ensure corporate performance is maximised and sustained."

Survey Findings

1. *Many finance organisations are ill equipped to excel in value-adding activities.* It is easy to assume that we know what that means, and yet the survey reported that very few of us do.

2. *Branding the company as a career destination for finance professionals is critical for attracting talent.* Few companies do this well.

3. *Many finance organisations do not capitalise on the graduate pool.*

4. *Career development is critical to those individuals who are career-focused.* Yet many companies keep finance people from pursuing learning or growth opportunities outside the management accounting function.

5. *Those with CFO ambitions need to take deliberate career steps and gain diverse business experiences.*

6. *Few finance organisations have developed proactive or innovative strategies to attract, develop and retain talent.*

The CFO's Current Challenges

The survey identified six challenges that CFOs face and the best ways to resolve those challenges.

1. Many accounting teams remain in a vacuum in which they deliver numbers but do not use the information to create value.

   Solution—The CFO must take specific action to turn his or her team's numbers into something valued by others.

2. Of the finance team's competency deficiencies, the abilities to be strategists and catalysts are the most glaring.

   Solution—The CFO must undertake a resource review of his or her team's talent needs and abilities.

3. The CFO rarely knows the types of talent needed and where to find those people.

   Solution—The CFO must create structures, then seek out and recruit management accounting talent wherever it exists.

4. The entire accounting group has trouble recognising talent.

   Solution—The CFO and team must hire people who have a value creation mindset.

5. The CFO does not assist his or her employees in finding experiences outside finance.

   Solution—The CFO should create or identify leadership development opportunities for his or her employees wherever they exist in the organisation.

6. The CFO typically relies on comfortable or traditional methods for assessing talent.

   Solution—The CFO must find additional ways to assess a person's potential, in partnership with the human resource department.

The views expressed in the previous section are drawn from a research project conducted by Economist Intelligence Unit in collaboration with the Deloitte Touche Tohmatsu, May 2007.

View 4—The Superstar CFO: Optimising an Increasingly Complex Role

The CFO who helps the organisation become successful operationally garners great rewards for himself or herself.

Intense Pressure

"Chief financial officers are under greater pressure, scrutiny, and accountability in companies large and small. The demands of both internal and external stakeholders continue to expand, and seemingly everyone expects more from companies and their finance function. The stakeholders look to the CFO for his or her unique understanding of

- company performance,
- business strategy,
- value-creation, and
- risk."

This study was undertaken to determine how the CFO currently deals with these increased pressures and to discover the attributes of highly successful CFOs.

Superstar Status Defined

A senior financial executive at a manufacturer said, "Extraordinary CFOs know no boundaries. They participate in the management and optimisation of the assets of the company—both physical and human." Superstar CFOs can be recognised by the following four traits. They

1. take ultimate responsibility for finance's efforts and results,
2. closely work with other parts of the organisation,
3. become a process expert and adviser, and
4. take responsibility for the integrity of the company's process and controls.

The CFO is more likely to excel as a leader of the finance function and demonstrate personal leadership by

- being both a navigator and a copilot,
- building consensus,
- inspiring confidence, and
- making decisions authoritatively.

The CFO's Achilles' Heel

The people who employ CFOs say that what most undermines their effectiveness is their spending too much time on management accounting's regular work. CFOs must develop a team who can take on these tactical matters so that they can focus their attention on mission-critical work.

The views expressed in the previous section are drawn from a research project by CFO Research Services in collaboration with SAP, May 2007.

View 5—CFOs and the Talent Gap: Does Finance Have the Right People?

Increasingly, business leaders see the competition for talent as the most significant global trend facing their companies.

Your Talent Gap

Corporate finance is on the forefront of today's fierce competition for talent. The following are causes for a shortage of qualified accounting people:

- The highly specialised and technical requirements of the job

- The globalisation of business, leading to more complexity

- Organisations reporting more on nonfinancial matters instead of financial ones

- Finance as the hub of company data that must provide forward-looking analysis for sound decision making

Solutions to Have the Right People
Tactic 1

As the leaders of talent management on our team, CFOs must better explain to candidates the role management accounting plays. They must help those they hire understand that management accounting is a springboard to many other career paths.

Tactic 2

The CFO must expand the use of tools beyond what he or she is comfortable with in order to both assess and develop talent. For example, appraisals from the line manager are good indicators of an employee's ability to provide the insights that operational people need. Some other tools a CFO can rely on include the following:

- 360° feedback

- Mentoring

- Coaching

- Succession planning

- Altering the team's incentive plans

Tactic 3

The best tactic the CFO can employ for better talent management is to seek out and obtain internal appreciation for the work that his or her people do. This helps the team improve the services it provides.

The views expressed in the previous section are drawn from a research project by CFO Research Services in collaboration with Microsoft, May 2008.

View 6—Preparing Finance Staff for the Future

The head of the management accounting team is in the midst of a longstanding effort to transform finance from a processor of data, to an organiser of information, to a true business partner and performance leader.

Prepare to Be Great

The survey in this report addresses the question of how the accounting function and leader of finance can prepare his or her staff to become true business partners and performance leaders. The survey uncovered a major barrier: the lack of well-rounded business, technology and even technical skills among finance employees. This barrier has become very difficult to overcome.

Survey Findings

1. *Although many large organisations offer formal training to management accountants, companies are more likely to use informal training.* According to those surveyed, ad hoc training is valuable and low-cost; however, it is inconsistent and neither continuous nor measurable.

2. *Formal training programmes most often emphasise technical accounting skills rather than analytical skills.* For organisations that have such programmes for the finance team, the training was described as lacking breadth and depth because of an over-emphasis on technical accounting and not enough attention to analysis, decision support and risk management. Formal training can suffer from being narrowly focused and not involving collaboration and partnering.

3. *CFOs recognise the value of formal training, yet they fall short on providing it.* The lack of resources provided to the finance function is the major cause. Another concern is the concentration on only tactical topics and the fact that only two specific employee groups get trained: (*a*) the newly hired and (*b*) those who show leadership potential.

4. *The top priorities for employee development and improvement include (a) increased emphasis on leadership skills and (b) building a closer connection between those skills and the organisation's needs.* The CFOs who responded believe that any training to finance must be tied into real-world and business-related issues and problems. In other words, management accounting's training must be tailored, not generic.

5. *The top barriers to improving employees' skills are competing priorities within both finance and the organisation at large.* CFOs said that it is much more difficult to provide necessary training for their employees if their organisation does not believe that training is critical for its success.

The Value of Training

"One of the most prominent themes to emerge from this research was the connection CFOs see between formal training programmes and career enhancement. They don't view formal training as a distraction" or as a remedial action for underperformers.

The views expressed in the previous section are drawn from a research project by CFO Research Services in collaboration with ACS, November 2007.

View 7—The Right Stuff: Leadership in Finance

Now, more than ever, finance leaders have the opportunity to guide and influence their organisations.

Continuing Pressure

This research project was "undertaken to examine the state of the finance profession from the perspective of senior finance executives" and found that, at least in the United States, management accountants "are acutely pressured by increased responsibility and heightened accountability. The research found that finance departments are not only under pressure to manage financial compliance, processes, and controls in environments of intense regulatory scrutiny, but also increasingly accountable for business performance."

However, the CFO has not been given adequate resources to respond to these pressures. What skills does the CFO need to meet these pressures?

Our Crucial Skills

Although this situation is difficult for many, it is also an opportunity for us, because the CFO is considered to be a major influence over both finance and the business in general. This role requires both technical skills and soft skills—complex management and leadership—in these specific areas:

- Collaboration
- Negotiation
- Communication

Those who responded to the survey said most often that the nuanced interpersonal skills, such as decision making, collaboration and flexibility, are necessary for their own success and to meet these demands and pressures. The skills that the CFOs defined as crucial are also those required for leadership effectiveness. Nevertheless, CFOs rated themselves higher on getting their traditional work done and lower on dealing with organisational politics.

Tactics to Enhance Your Leadership Abilities

When asked about specific suggestions for the person who wants to become a better leader of finance, these six suggestions came to the forefront:

1. Obtain ongoing feedback
2. Seek out new experiences
3. Provide mentoring and training to others
4. Take courses on leadership
5. Seek out and maintain connections
6. Spend time doing personal reflection and self-analysis

These six skills that contribute to our success mirror the corporate culture that our employers need in order to foster our organisation's lasting success and sustainability.

The views expressed in the previous section are drawn from a research project by CFO Research Services in collaboration with Tatum, March 2008.

View 8—Bean Counter to Business Leader: The Changing Role of the CFO

CFOs have a golden opportunity to show that they are true business leaders.

No More Beans

The role of the CFO is evolving, but due to the daily and never-ending pressures of closings, reporting, meeting deadlines and the sea of other finance duties, a strong tendency still exists for the CFO to act as the "chief bean counter." The white paper reviewed in this section encourages CFOs to shed this title in the following ways:

1. Improve Your Visibility by Turning Data Into Better Business Decisions

CFOs must create a common platform for the data they control so that everyone knows both the source and integrity of the numbers—financial and nonfinancial. They must have high quality data that is shared and fosters sound business decisions.

2. Create Quick Wins

CFOs and their team should work on low hanging fruit and focus their efforts on the sharpest pains. One way to help a team get quick wins is to have better forecasting techniques and share reliable data with others.

3. Design the Right Roadmap

CFOs must establish an accurate roadmap for their team and establish specific and achievable goals with three different time frames. Three different time frames for goals help you to be strategic but not neglect the tactical part of your job:

- Long-term
- Mid-term
- Short-term

4. Empower the Organisation

As CFO, your responsibility is to empower the organisation by

- distributing information,
- balancing centralisation with authority,
- providing tools,
- providing data with analysis, and
- fostering a performance culture.

However, you cannot implement this fourth strategy alone. The entire leadership team helps to establish a performance-sensitive culture, which requires each member to

- collaborate,
- convince others,
- negotiate,
- inspire others, and
- listen.

The views expressed in the previous section are drawn from a BPM Partners white paper, July 2009.

What do the eight trends and findings previously discussed say about you and what you need to accomplish or change in the next 12 months?

Universal Theme No. 2: Our Performance Gap

Another theme to take away from these eight different views about the CFOs' future has to do with the gap between how CFOs are performing now and how they need to be performing. This performance gap has the following multiple dimensions:

1. Our own skill level

2. Our team's performance level

3. How we develop future management accountant

4. The quality of services that we provide to our customers

As the head of the management accounting function, you cannot afford to stay in this performance gap very long because the longer you stay there, the quicker you lose the credibility and respect you have with your employer and with your peers on the management team. Therefore, it is vital to quickly determine where you and your team have performance gaps and spend the next 12 months resolving them.

Universal Theme No. 3: The Collaborative Partnership

Another theme in many of the studies is our relationship with people in the operational side of our organisations. Management accounting is not only a service provider to them, but also a partner with them. Management accountants must collaborate with them in order to provide the services that they require from the accountants to do their jobs. Nearly every study discussed how CFOs must create a culture of collaboration, not only within the organisation but also within their team. This means that every member of their team must know how to collaborate.

As with any partnership, each side has obligations and responsibilities. The following chart shows these obligations. Ours are on the left side, and the obligations of the people we serve are on the right. As head of the management accounting function, your responsibility is to instil into each member of your team the importance of living up to his or her obligations. As a member of the organisation's leadership body, your responsibility is to help the operational side of the business understand their obligations to us.

Mutual Obligations

Table 1-1 represents a contrast between the management accounting team's obligations and the operational team's obligations. Notice as you review this table how much we need each other's support.

Table 1-1: Management Accounting vs. Operations Team Obligations

MANAGEMENT ACCOUNTING OBLIGATIONS	OPERATION'S OBLIGATIONS
Tell the truth	Listen to the truth
Know the business	Understand the basics of finance
Spend time in operations	Spend time meeting with finance
Support operations	Support finance
Create insight	Believe in the numbers
Offer ideas to operations	Offer suggestions to finance
Communicate openly	Communicate needs to finance
Communicate often with operations	Communicate often with finance
Speak and write in operational terms	Learn basic finance terms and concepts
Help executives hold operations people accountable	Be accountable for the results
Provide narratives	Use finance's information in day-to-day decisions
Provide simple, concise and to-the-point information	Provide high quality operational data to finance
Predict the future	Predict the future
Support operations in making good decisions	Rely on finance for decision making purposes
Analyse current and future risk	Analyse risk with finance's help
Create transparency with your data	Be transparent in your decisions and data sources

Solution No. 1—How to Overcome the Performance Gap

Here are nine specific actions that you can take to help overcome your own performance gap:

1. Select your own mentor or coach and use that person to turn your weaknesses or blind spots into strengths.

2. Regularly survey the people you serve to find out how they view your current level of service and performance. Use this valuable feedback to improve.

3. Every month, conduct a team self-analysis, in the form of Plus-Delta, to find out what you have done well and what you must change. Use this valuable feedback to improve.

4. Make every effort to attend important meetings that occur around the organisation, especially those that do not involve financial issues. Use these events as opportunities to collaborate.

5. Encourage the members of your management accounting team to spend time with their customers as part of their regular responsibilities. Use these interactions as opportunities to collaborate.

6. Spend at least two hours each week thinking strategically and setting goals for the short-term, medium-term and long-term.

7. Spend time in every staff meeting brainstorming additional ways to provide value-added services to your team's customers. Use this as an opportunity to collaborate.

8. Discourage members of your finance team from speaking in accounting jargon and encourage them to use the same words and phrases that operational people use.

9. Write a development and training plan for every member of your team. Include areas in which the team member is deficient and needs to improve. Include those skills in which he or she excels so he or she can teach those skills to other team members.

Your turn: offer your own suggestions for overcoming your expectations gap.

Solution No. 2—How to Prepare for Tomorrow

As a wise professional, you know that to be prepared for the unknown future, you need to start preparing yourself today.

Answer This Question:

What does the controller or CFO need to do to become the visible and influential leader of this major transition?

2

STEP 2: BECOME AN EFFECTIVE COACH

"You cannot lead if you don't believe."

—Professor C.K. Prahalad of the University of Michigan Business School

Thankfully, the business world has made strides in moving away from a command and control form of leadership. This obsolete and ineffective method is being replaced by a coaching leadership style. A majority of today's most successful CEOs describe themselves as coaches first and managers second.

In this second step, we begin by looking at coaching at the individual level and move on to how the skill also applies at the organisational level. You will discover that coaching is something that you may be already doing as a supervisor. Do not assume that coaching is a soft skill; in fact, it is a mix of both technical and people skills combined in a unique fashion that produces great results for the leader who believes in and utilises coaching.

After reading this chapter, you should be able to

- know if you have the skills necessary to be an effective coach.

- apply the best practice of a position description to get greater results.

- coach a friend through a difficult situation.

- develop into a powerful coach for your organisation.

COACHING IN A NUTSHELL

We turn to a coach when we want to improve a specific skill or talent and are unable to do it on our own.

The coach is someone who is skilled in the area and can provide guided help so CFOs will end up in a better place than they are now. Being a coach in business is similar to coaching in sports; you are administering skill-based practice so that the person can reach a specific outcome. The coach's job is to help the coachee see the obstacles that are preventing him or her from being successful and to jump-start the momentum needed to reach a goal. Being a successful coach is extremely satisfying and gratifying.

COACHING AT THE INDIVIDUAL LEVEL

The Skill of Coaching

Coaching is personalised, individualised training and support given to someone. It is building a continual relationship between the coach and the person being coached.

Coaching is not

- controlling,
- managing,
- micromanaging, or
- supervising.

Coaching is dramatically more challenging, yet rewarding, than the out-of-date command and control method for managing people. In command and control the leader dictates the rules and tasks while adhering to a strict chain of command. Employees are not allowed to question these "orders" and can communicate with the leader only via established formal channels of communication. Because today's business organisation is flatter and has fewer manager and supervisor positions, it is incumbent that you create and retain a personal connection with each employee who directly or indirectly reports to you. This is why coaching is so important and necessary to be a successful controller or CFO.

In coaching, the leader works each day to foster a personal and open relationship with each employee so that these human assets feel that they can come to you and tell you the truth when things are going well or going poorly. The communication channels used in coaching are more informal and dependent on continuous face-to-face interactions. If you are a good coach, you will find that employees trust you and believe in you and will do everything they can to ensure that you are successful. This occurs because you have repeatedly demonstrated to your employees that you believe they are valuable and want them to succeed.

Coaching is not controlling because you are the guide who allows your employees to determine the agenda and goals.

Coaching is not managing because you are using your knowledge and insights to help your employees come into their own wisdom.

Coaching is not micromanaging because you are not doing the work, but instead trusting your employees and letting them successfully stumble so they quickly learn to succeed.

Coaching is not supervising, because you can coach anybody; it does not need to be an employee. You can coach a boss, a colleague, a friend or even a stranger. The process of coaching is consistent and, once you master it, you will find many ways to use it to help others become successful and effective.

For the rest of this book, the term *coachee* refers to the person you are coaching in order to emphasise the importance of applying the skill of coaching beyond those for whom you are responsible.

Accountability Factor in Coaching

Because, as a leader, you are not commanding or demanding that your employees get the work done in the way that you want it done, you may feel that you will spend all your time micromanaging what employees do and say. This is not true. If you are a good coach, you will be transferring accountability for results to each of the employees whom you coach. That is what the coach does best—transfer accountability for success back into the hands of the coachee.

As you coach people and establish a relationship of trust, you offer suggestions and ideas to help them be more productive and make their work life easier. Then the actual work is performed by the employee, who feels accountable to you for completing what he or she promised to do and meeting the quality you expect. If employees do not perform according to your expectations, they will feel embarrassed because you placed your trust in them and they let you down.

In the coaching relationship, you guide and shape the coachee's behaviours in subtle and specific ways. You do this for the benefit of both the organisation and the employee, thereby requiring that you approach the relationship with sincerity and honour. You hold no hidden agenda. In effect, as coach, you are creating an environment in which the people who work for you want to win, yearn to feel successful and enjoy doing their best.

Notice that a leader who uses the dictatorial command and control method of getting others to do the work will never create an environment in which people feel successful or care enough to win. Similarly, the leader who uses micromanaging to ensure that employees do everything right will never create an environment in which people enjoy doing their best or are accountable for their own successes and failures.

Specific Skills of a True Coach

- Teaching   _____
- Counselling   _____
- Guiding   _____
- Learning   _____
- Sharing   _____
- Questioning   _____
- Relating   _____
- Listening   _____
- Intuitiveness   _____
- Creativity   _____

Grade yourself on each skill, using this scale:

1 – I don't have or practise the skill.

2 – I have some of the skill.

3 – I probably am average in relation to the skill.

4 – I get good results when I use the skill.

5 – I improved an employee's performance using the skill.

Coaching Skills Defined

"The manager's daily challenge is to enable workers to become responsible by extending trust, mentoring, being receptive to new ideas, encourage risk-taking, giving credit, and telling uncompromising truth."

—Rob Lebow, Professional Coach

Teaching and Training

In coaching, teaching is somewhat akin to the experiences we had with our teachers in school. The teacher would carefully explain to us the new skill and help us to understand why it was important for us to learn that skill. In a coaching session, you are teaching the person what he or she needs to know and explaining the context so that he or she understands the new information. To ensure that the coachee understands the applicability of the new information, you also train him or her on how to apply it and when.

Counselling

In your experiences as a supervisor, you know that some employees need or want you to hold their hand as you guide them through a difficult situation. In coaching, you often act as a counsellor or sage who dispenses advice and suggestions. In your role as a coach, you will often need to be the person who gives the employee tough love, which also falls under the skill of counselling.

Guiding

A critical role the coach plays in getting someone to improve his or her performance or to change a habit is to be the guide. See this as being the Sherpa for someone who is climbing Mount Everest for the first time. You are unveiling the future path that the person could and hopefully will take in order to become better. In everything that you do as a coach, whether it be offering advice and counsel or holding the person accountable, you will ultimately guide that person to a better place.

Learning

One of the valuable traits that a good coach displays is the willingness to learn. You learn from the relationship with your coachee, from the wisdom of your own words and from the examples of other leaders. Coaches are not expected to know everything, so you must commit to lifelong learning by reading books and studying. Learn about successful leaders, great organisations and best practices. As you develop the relationship with the coachee, you will learn things about that person and about yourself.

Sharing

One of the things that coaches do very well is to share the wisdom of their own experience with the coachee. Coaches are not expected to be perfect, and the more mistakes you have made, the more real and honest you will appear to your coachee. Hopefully, you have learned some valuable lessons from your experiences, especially your mistakes, that you can pass on to those travelling the same path as you.

Questioning

The most powerful tool that the coach has available is the use of thoughtful questioning. Instead of relying on declarative statements, a good coach uses questions to open the coachee's eyes and mind to new possibilities. Very often the person you are coaching cannot clearly see or is so focused on what is not working that he or she misses what is working. In addition, because of your wisdom and experiences you clearly see where the person needs to get to and the path for getting there. But if you give away all the answers, the coachee misses out on the experience of finding his or her own way. So to be an effective coach you use questions—open-ended and pointed—to get the coachee to create the conclusions that will help him or her reach the desired outcome.

Relating

One of the strongest ways that coaches build the relationship of trust is to use analogies, examples and stories to get their point across. That means you must walk in the shoes of the coachee and see the world through his or her eyes. Quite often that means you will need to mentally and emotionally understand where the coachee is now and then use this information to create an example for the person to understand the bigger picture. The coach will use examples and stories from many different sources, which constantly requires the coach to be learning and growing.

Listening

Along with the skill of questioning, as a coach you will intensively rely on the ability to listen with your ears, your eyes and your intuition. If the person you are coaching could clearly see the obstacle in question, he or she would not need a coach. Because the coachee cannot see the path without filters, he or she may focus only on the obstacles. This inability to see beyond an obstacle causes great distress and negative emotion in the coachee. He or she will circle around the issue, resist or deny that anything is wrong. The coach's job is to listen to what is said and unsaid in order to get a sense of what is really stopping the person, which most of the time will be an unwillingness to face up to fear.

Using Intuition

Every one of us is born with strong intuitive abilities. It is through our life's experiences that we learn either to rely on our intuition or to deny its existence. Accountants are famous for denying that they have intuition. Successful coaches recognise the importance of their intuition and use it in building the coachee relationship.

As a coach you will not rely on intuition all the time; instead, it will flow in and out during your discussions and interactions with the coachee. These are moments when an "Aha" occurs. In such a moment of clarity you may be tempted to give the person the answer instead of taking the time to draw it out with questions.

Remember that your intuition is both an asset and your ally for being an effective coach.

Creativity

The creativity that the coach needs to be successful in getting others to change is one of being open-minded to new possibilities and new ways of seeing life. This skill works hand-in-hand with your intuition. Creativity comes to fruition when you think of tools, methods or processes that the coachee can use to go from being stuck to succeeding.

Example

The person you are coaching is holding on to the past, stuck on some negative interaction with a coworker from five years ago. Your intuition tells you that if the employee can get beyond that negative emotion he will be more proactive in dealing with co-worker conflict. You think of a creative exercise and ask the employee to do the following:

"Write down on a piece of paper the event as you remember it. Once it is detailed, take that piece of paper and stick it in an ashtray. Then set it on fire."

This activity may sound strange, but it may lead the employee to realise he can move beyond this limiting event he obsesses about and release his fear.

Therefore, as coach, it is incumbent on you to constantly think of methods that the coachee can use to progress towards a goal, even though you may feel the method is unorthodox.

COACHING AT THE ORGANISATIONAL LEVEL

Coaching at the organisational level requires the controller to be the conscience of their firm. You must be the person who is willing to raise issues and counsel other leaders on the viability of their goals, plans and policies. You must be seen as the professional leader who does not have any biases or an agenda other than the organisation's success.

Notably, the skills that you use in coaching an individual are the same ones you use in being a coach at the organisational level. You must be able to listen beyond the words, use questions to open up dialogue, build trust between yourself and your colleagues, and ultimately guide people's thinking and behaviours. Let us recap those skills.

Teaching and Training

As the controller or CFO, you are constantly teaching others about the nuances of finance, accounting and business management. As you discovered in the view of the CFO in the future, our position is moving toward that of a constant trainer.

Counselling

You will need to hold the hands of other leaders and colleagues as you guide them through difficult situations and tough decisions. In coaching at the organisational level, you will often act as a wise person who dispenses advice and suggestions. And you will often need to dispense advice people may not want to hear.

Guiding

Just as in coaching the individual, you must guide the actions and decisions of other leaders as they make choices and decisions. Although it would be nice if every leader in your organisation had integrity, that is not always the case. Once you choose to be the controller or CFO, you must be willing to shape other leaders' behaviours and decisions so that they stay focused on solutions and plans that benefit the customer, the organisation and its stakeholders rather than themselves.

Learning

Although you are an accomplished professional, you still have many things to learn. By keeping an open mind and knowing that you can learn from the examples of other leadership team members, you will ensure your future success and discover that many other avenues exist to channel your talents in the organisation. Some controllers use their experiences and knowledge to become CEOs, venture capitalists, hedge fund managers, niche consultants and operations executives. The controller's job is a launching pad that opens the door to the unlimited opportunities available to the person who is willing to stretch beyond what is comfortable and predictable.

Sharing

Just as in coaching the individual, you will share your insights and wisdom with others in the form of stories, examples and analogies.

Questioning

One of a CFO's more powerful tools is the use of thoughtful questioning. Instead of relying on declarative statements, a good leader uses questions to open people's eyes and minds to new possibilities. Very often, executives and managers are so focused on their agenda that they cannot see beyond it. Because of your wisdom and experiences, you clearly see what the leadership team needs to do to accomplish its strategic initiatives. Therefore, to be an effective CFO you must acquire the habit of using questions—open-ended and probing—to lead the leadership team to create the conclusions that will help it reach the organisation's goals.

Relating

One of the strongest ways that you, the controller, builds bridges and fosters relationships of trust is to use analogies, examples and stories to get your point across. This means you must speak at the same level of the coachee. The controller or coach will use examples and stories from many different sources. This constantly requires you to be listening, learning and growing.

Listening

Along with the skill of questioning, as the organisation's internal coach you will intensely rely on the ability to listen with your ears, your eyes and your intuition. Managers with hidden agendas or hubris will rarely speak clearly and address the issue. Instead they will circle around the issue. They will resist. They will deny that anything is wrong. Your job is to listen to what is said and unsaid in order to get a sense of what the person is not saying or is trying to hide. By listening carefully and using questions, you become more the organisational conscience as you bring forth those things that need to be expressed and brought out into the open.

Using Intuition

Just as in coaching the individual, over time you will develop a keen sense of what to say and what not to say. This is sometimes called business sense but is, in fact, your intuition. It is wisdom you hone from your experiences both within the organisation and from without. Remember that your intuition is both an asset and your ally for being an effective controller or CFO.

Creativity

The creativity that the CFO needs to be successful in getting others to change is that of being open-minded to new possibilities. This skill works hand-in-hand with your intuition. Your creativity comes into fruition when you think of tools, methods or processes that the organisation and other leaders can use to remove obstacles that hinder execution of plans.

Therefore, as CFO it is vital that you be constantly thinking of tools and best practices that the leadership team can use to make progress toward corporate goals and strategic initiatives.

CONTROLLER AND CFO BEST PRACTICE: POSITION DESCRIPTION

A position description is much more than a typical job description. It is a tool that helps you to fully define a job and emphasise what the organisation wants—results.

Elements of the Position Description

While a job description is something every controller or CFO and member of her team should have, the position description will enable the leading-edge leader of finance to be very successful. This assurance comes from proactively defining your role within the company using the following elements:

- **Qualifications** for the job
- **Expected results** from the employee
- **Impact** of the job on the organisation
- **Authority levels** granted with the position
- **Specific difficulties** the person may have
- **Interpersonal relationships,** within and without
- Functional **job duties**
- Any other key items necessary for the employee to succeed

A typical job description concentrates on the role's duties, while the focal point of the position description is on the expected results. By emphasising results, you eliminate the need to include every conceivable task into the job description.

This approach is useful when used on the marginally successful employee who hides under the reasoning: "But that task is not in my job description." By defining what you expect of your employees, you eliminate this popular excuse and self-limiting belief.

Expected Results

Define and get your supervisor's agreement on the desired outcomes before you get deep into the job. This action helps you stay focused and enforces personal accountability.

Impact on the Organisation

You agree with your employer as to obtaining the resources you need so that you can make the desired impact and achieve the expected results. This clarification helps in your leadership and conscience roles.

Authority Levels

You understand what decisions you can and cannot make and ask for those that will support you in rendering the expected results. This definition helps you know what is really important.

Special Difficulties

You spell out those things which could limit your ability to get quick or lasting results, like needing to upgrade the technical skills of your existing staff or having to invest in new technology. This section helps you and your supervisor or employer be mutually accountable to each other.

Interpersonal Relationships

You agree with your employer as to the people that you have responsibility for, whom you regularly communicate with, and where you fit into the organisation's structure. This agreement helps you to keep your eyes on the big picture.

Benefits of Using a Position Description

Why should you have a position description for yourself and each member of your team? The payoffs are numerous. A specific description

- communicates clear expectations to everyone,
- clarifies goals in advance,
- reduces overlaps and gaps among the many team members' duties and responsibilities,
- reduces uncertainty about what is expected,
- documents performance,
- shortens the learning curve for new employees, and
- gives a clear definition of the job requirements to any applicant.

Tips on Making the Position Description Effective

Expectations-Oriented

Every position description should focus on the results you expect from that specific employee. To ensure that the position description remains fresh and current, semiannually update every employee's position description or every time you conduct a performance evaluation, whichever comes first.

Proactive

Be sure to state the expected results in a proactive manner. This encourages your employee to take initiative and become more of a self-starter. Your role will gradually evolve into that of an encouraging coach rather than a supervisor.

Flexible

By focusing the employee's attention on expected results instead of duties, you automatically instil greater flexibility in the employee. If you want to develop employees who are proactive and seek out ways to add value, make each employee's position description flexible.

Broad

Today, ideal employees see the big picture, so it is important that you make the position description broad enough to cover more than what the employee is currently doing. By developing the position description with a wide variety of expectations, you instil in the employee the practice of looking toward future possibilities.

Brief

The ideal position description is only one and a half pages long. To the extent possible, create a position description that is no more than two pages. If you can get the position description on one page, you will make it even more effective and memorable. The length will depend on how many duties you include. Remember, the more you detail the expected results, the less you need to spell out the specific duties. See figure 2-1 for the position description format.

Figure 2-1: Success Unlimited Position Description Format

Name of Incumbent _____   Position _____

Salary Grade _____   Department/Team _____

Qualifications: Education, experience, specialised knowledge or skills. Personal qualities are not considered legitimate qualifications.

> "4-year accounting degree with 2 to 4 years' experience at supervisor level. ACMA, FCMA, or CPA. One year experience in percentage-of-completion cost accounting."

Expected Results: Measurable standards of performance such as cost reduction or project deadlines.

> "Implement computerisation of General Ledger before July 1st."

Impact: Company assets for which the employee is accountable including people, money, equipment, expense limits, or sales.

> "Lead a team of 10 professionals and manage a departmental budget of $500,000."

Authority: Limitations (if any) on decisions made, approvals given, contract signing, hiring and firing.

> "Accounts payable invoice approval up to $5,000. Travel expense voucher approval up to $1,000."

Principal Duties: Major functional responsibilities.

> "Establish and monitor budgets for all division departments."

Special Difficulties: Problems or obstacles the employee must overcome in achieving goals and producing expected results.

> "Most action items are subject to strict deadline pressure."

Interpersonal Relationships: Insiders and outsiders the employee routinely interacts with such as auditors, government agencies, colleagues, customers or vendors.

> "Principal point of contact with our external auditors and tax authorities."

An example of a position description is presented on the following pages.

Position Description for a General Accounting Assistant

Qualifications

The person who fills this position will have a minimum of two years' entry-level accounting experience or a college education. He or she will have the interpersonal skills and problem solving experience expected of a professional. His or her technical knowledge will include, at a minimum, usage of PC-based computer systems and related applications as well as knowledge and usage of spreadsheet software, e-mail, Internet searches and databases.

Expected Results

Within nine months of being on the job, the employee will have accomplished these goals:

- Measurable improvements in accounts receivable collections reducing DSO (day's sales outstanding) from the current 60 days to 35 days
- After completing cross-training, have a good understanding of the duties and functions of accounts payable and payroll processing
- Take over maintenance of the general ledger and preparation of related internal report package from the controller

Principle Duties

- Timely collection of accounts receivable, including follow-up and documentation
- Precise monthly inventory reconciliations
- Precise monthly reconciliation of bank accounts
- Detailed and accurate analysis of general ledger accounts and preparation of work papers
- Cross-training and understanding of duties in the following areas:
    - Accounts payable processing and transactions, for example, coding, processing payments and so forth
    - Cash receipts processing and transactions, for example, coding, posting, reconciliation and so forth
    - Sales processing and transactions, for example, invoicing, summarising, posting and so forth
    - Payroll processing and transactions, for example, data entry, tax filings and deposits, and so forth
    - Other accounting related duties and special projects as assigned and delegated

Special Difficulties

- Quickly learning a complex accounting system
- Working with a difficult accounting software package

Interpersonal Relationships

- Direct supervisor will be the controller
- Task supervisors will be a staff accountant and the AP specialist whenever cross-training and working within that person's area of responsibility
- Person will have daily contact with customers, bank employees and company employees

Evaluation and Feedback

Quarterly performance evaluations will be made on the goals defined in the "Expected Results" section and on the employee's learning curve in the following areas:

- Technical skills and problem solving skills
- People skills
- Professionalism
- Communication skills
- Speed in completion of cross-training
- Comprehension of training
- Enthusiasm
- Proactiveness
- Flexibility
- Willingness to learn

Exercise: Brian—Part 1

In the following activity, you will examine specific challenges that Brian faces and then complete Brian's position description.

Case Study Background Information

Brian, Your Friend

Brian is the controller and acting CFO of an organisation located in a small community. The company Brian works for could be described as a mini-conglomerate or informal private equity fund.

Brian's Employer

Known as R & K Enterprises, the organisation is a holding company of small businesses owned by two families. The organisation itself is too big to qualify as a small business. In the latest count, taken at end of the most recent fiscal year, this organisation comprises 33 different enterprises or entities divided up into 14 business units or profit centres, detailed as follows.

	R & K'S BUSINESS UNITS (# OF ENTITIES)	NET REVENUE (MILLIONS)	EMPLOYEES
1	Manufacturing (3)	$74	98
2	Retail (4)	$61	27
3	Wholesale (2)	$32	16
4	Fast food and restaurant franchises (7)	$12	117
5	Mining/Mineral Rights (2)	$5	5
6	Land and building holdings—apartments (5)	$4	13

	R & K'S BUSINESS UNITS (# OF ENTITIES)	NET REVENUE (MILLIONS	EMPLOYEES
7	Land and building sales (1)	$4	2
8	Equipment rentals (2)	$3	6
9	Land and building development (1)	$3	2
10	New car dealership (1)	$2	8
11	Land and building holdings—commercial (2)	$2	4
12	Electrical contracting (1)	$1	3
13	Landscaping (1)	$1	4
14	Family Trust (1)	N/A	2
	Total Gross Revenues—last fiscal year	**$204**	
	Total headcount, today		**307**

The Ownership

Ruwan and Kimberley, the primary owners, are unsophisticated serial entrepreneurs. Serial entrepreneurs start or buy a business, get it successfully running as a standalone enterprise, and then lose interest and go after another idea. Many members of their respective families are involved in the various businesses.

Examples of Interrelations

Ruwan's wife is the agent/broker and serves as managing director of the four land and building business units.

Kimberley's son is an electrical contractor and a managing director for two business units.

Kimberley's nephew is the managing director of the landscaping business.

These three businesses and others serve as vendors to many of the R & K entities.

A family trust was set up by their accountants more than 20 years ago purely as a tax deferral mechanism and buy-sell vehicle should one of the principals die prematurely.

Brian's Team

Brian directly reports to and works for the owners as the main financial decision maker and as a primary trustee. The owners prefer to centralise most of the accounting and administrative duplicative functions in R & K's corporate offices, housed in one of the commercial buildings they own. Brian's shared-services staff is listed as follows. The larger enterprises have either bookkeepers or accountants on site.

BRIAN'S TEAM IN CORPORATE	
Accounts payable	6
Cash management and applications	7
Purchasing support	2
General ledger accountants	3
Business unit accountants	4
Cost accounting	4

Continued on p.34

BRIAN'S TEAM IN CORPORATE	
Accounting assistants	5
Technical support (coordinates with IT)	2
Assistant controller	2
IT staff	5
Paralegal bookkeepers for family trust	2
Corporate Accounting Staff	**42**
BRIAN'S TEAM OUTSIDE CORPORATE	
On site staff in business units	13
Brian's Team	**55**

All told, Brian directly supervises 42 people. Counting the other 13 professionals he influences, his total management breadth is 55 employees.

Brian's Role

In addition to these accounting duties, Brian serves as internal auditor and internal consultant to the managers of the different business units. This latter role is important because while both Kimberley and Ruwan like to work in the business, they hate working *on* the business.

Fortunately, Brian is not responsible for human resources. Due to the large size of the workforce and frequent turnover, especially in the manufacturing, retail and fast food units, human resources is competently handled by a fully staffed and professionally run team.

Other Leaders

Because the managing director of each unit is empowered to run that business as they see fit, few of them have any leadership or management training. Universally, they perform well at operations, but poorly at management.

Brian's Leadership Challenges

Issue 1: Brian Is Not Taken Seriously

Owners Ruwan and Kimberley regularly ignore Brian's ideas for improvements.

Example 1
Brian suggested that all the land and building entities be combined into one business unit and be managed by an experienced land and building professional. Doing so would accomplish the following:

Save both state and federal income taxes

Allow Brian to renegotiate with various lenders, possibly getting better terms and a larger credit line

Allow Ruwan more time to focus his efforts on selling and leasing, thus increasing revenue

---

> **Example 2**
>
> Brian suggested that the company hold a semi-annual retreat for all of the managing directors and other managers so that Ruwan and Kimberley could work on the big picture, explain their vision and get everyone's buy-in. This meeting would accomplish the following:
>
> Shorten and improve both the budget and goal-setting process
>
> Make it easy for both Ruwan and Kimberley to focus on the big picture two times a year
>
> Strengthen all the managing directors' leadership skills

> **Example 3**
>
> Brian wants to install a new performance measurement system that will allow the leadership group to better measure the success of each business entity and help R & K hold the managing directors accountable. The system will also facilitate giving Ruwan and Kimberley objective data that will help them decide when to sell a business from their diverse portfolio.
>
> Brian has asked Ruwan's and Kimberley's independent accountant, Ahsan, to address issues like these. Ahsan likes tax and accounting problems but avoids people and family politics issues. Due to their long-standing and cosy relationship, Ahsan does whatever Ruwan or Kimberley ask him to do.

To date, all of Brian's ideas have fallen on deaf ears.

Issue 2: The Firm Is in a Death Spiral

While the enterprise looks successful on paper, Brian believes that it is slowly dying. Brian has isolated three specific reasons for this deterioration:

1. *Growing debt used to buy questionable businesses*—Long-term debt has grown by 237% over the last 5 years, when many of their favoured businesses were acquired or started. The firm's banker, a long-time family friend, is nearing retirement, and Brian is concerned about the outcome of a more professional loan officer taking over their account.

2. *Lack of a viable exit plan*—Ruwan and Kimberley's existing exit plan, via the trust, is set up for inheritance taxes issues and not for continuity. If they cannot find a buyer who is willing to pay maximum value for the larger units, the enterprise will drastically drop in value because many of the favoured business entities have little value to anyone outside the family. Also, without Kimberley and Ruwan in the picture, nobody else is talented enough or committed enough to keep things running smoothly.

3. *Poor strategic leadership*—Due to his intense workload, Brian has been unable to persuade either Ruwan or Kimberley to spend more time working on the business. They manage their favourite pieces, but not the organisation as a whole.

Issue 3: They Hold Onto a Business Too Long Out of Ego

Every business unit, from manufacturing to land and building, is suffering due to both local and national economic woes. Next year's revenues are projected to drop overall by 25%–35%. Many of these units could have been sold for a high price years ago, but not today. Both Ruwan and Kimberley pride themselves as smart business people but ignore or diminish any bad or costly decisions.

Issue 4: They Have Severe Negative Cash Flows

The mining operations and land and building development efforts currently eat up more cash than they bring in. Brian appears to be the only one concerned about this situation.

Continued on p.36

Important Note

Resigning is not an option. Brian hopes to move into a COO role or maybe become the acting CEO of R & K if he can prove his worth to Ruwan and Kimberley. He is courageous and committed to seeing this matter through to the end, whatever that might be.

The following is an excerpt from Brian's recently developed position description.

R & K Enterprise Controller Position Description

Qualifications:

The competent professional filling this important management position will be the following:

An FCMA or CPA with at least seven years' experience in small closely held businesses

Someone with solid competency in cost accounting for mining, manufacturing, land and building, and restaurants

Knowledgeable in land and building development issues, including contracts and legal documentation

Experienced in the cash management of small business and multiple entities

Able to negotiate with bankers and other lenders

An expert in technology for small business and able to manage the IT infrastructure for different accounting and information systems

Experienced, three years or more, in mergers and acquisitions and divestitures

Bondable and able to serve as trustee for a family trust

Up-to-date on current tax regulations and family tax planning

Willing to work with the co-CEOs to establish a more professional approach to running the organisation

Serve as internal auditor and internal consultant to business unit managers

Interpersonal Relations:

Directly reports to Ruwan and Kimberley (co-CEOs)

Sits on the management committee, consisting of business unit general managers

Directly or indirectly supervises the entire shared-services staff

Coordinates functional responsibilities for finance, administrative and IT departments

Supports human resources group in setting personnel policies and practices and selecting benefit packages

Serves as independent trustee for family trust

Is primary contact with banker, accounting firm and legal counsel

Expected Results:

Create professional shared-service department consisting of administration, IT and finance so that employee turnover drops below 12%

Improve cash flows of the entire organisation by 10% the 1st year, 20% the 2nd year and 30% or more the 3rd year

Create an internal management reporting system that provides timely information on each business entity and the entire organisation

Reduce reporting process by 5 days over the next 18 months

Improve skills of all staff members so that each employee can assume more responsibilities as the enterprise expands

Establish ongoing cross-training for IT, finance and administrative positions so that necessary work can be completed during employee illnesses and holidays

Implement a job rotation process for all shared-service positions, if possible

Streamline processes so that the accounting function is handled with the fewest amount of personnel, decreasing the staff to employee ratio from 15% to 12%

Improve the internal controls of all entities and establish acceptable loss levels for each business unit

Develop a risk management programme for the entire enterprise in order to reduce insurance costs by at least 25%

Reduce the cost of employee benefits by 15% over the next 24 months

Improve the quality and speed of the annual planning process

Impact of the Job on the Organisation:

As a direct result of this position's responsibility and effectiveness, the organisation will have a conscientious leader who will assist in setting the tone for

- Risk-taking

- Synergy

- Responsibility

- Sharing costs

- Entrepreneurship

- Continuous growth

As a direct result of the position's responsibility and effectiveness, the shared-services function will be managed by an expert in accounting, finance, treasury, administration, personnel, mergers and acquisitions, and corporate taxation.

The family's trust account will be managed with the utmost accountability and prudence.

Principle Duties:

(Omitted)

Authority Levels:

(You complete this section.)

Continued on p.38

Special Difficulties:

(You complete this section.)

_____

_____

_____

_____

_____

Authority of Person to Act for the Company:

(You complete this section.)

_____

_____

_____

_____

_____

Special Difficulties of the Position:

(You complete this section.)

_____

_____

_____

_____

_____

_____

Exercise: Self-Test: How Well Do You Coach?

Instructions

Part 1: Perform this analysis, which will give you specific feedback on your coaching abilities, specifically what you are strong at and what you may choose to improve.

AS A COACH, I:	SELDOM	SOMETIMES	ALMOST ALWAYS
Capitalise on my employees' strengths.	1	2	3
Give my employees visibility to others.	1	2	3
Provide freedom for my employees to do their jobs.	1	2	3
Set specific standards of excellence.	1	2	3
Orient my employees to our values and strategies.	1	2	3
Hold my employees accountable.	1	2	3
Protect my employees from undue stress.	1	2	3
Encourage my employees when they are discouraged or are undertaking a new or difficult assignment.	1	2	3
Provide information about the organisation and my employees' role in attaining our goals.	1	2	3
Make my performance expectations and priorities clear.	1	2	3
Take time to build trust with each employee.	1	2	3
Provide appropriate training and support.	1	2	3
Solicit, listen and use ideas, even challenging ones.	1	2	3
View my employees as partners and critical to the success of our unit or team.	1	2	3
Serve as a good and visible role model.	1	2	3
Won't let my employee give up on him- or herself.	1	2	3
Do not divulge confidences or spread negativity.	1	2	3
Explain reasons for our decisions and give advance notice of changes whenever possible.	1	2	3
Provide my employees with regular and timely feedback about their job performance.	1	2	3
Give my employees credit, especially when they deserve it.	1	2	3
Totals for Each Column			
Grand Total			

Answer Key

If your Grand Total is:

50–60 *You are an excellent coach.*

40–49 *You are learning to be a coach.*

Below 40   *You need a personal coach yourself.*

Continued on p.40

Part 2: Answer These Questions

What areas do you feel that you are strong in and need to continue developing?

What areas do you feel you need to work on to improve your coaching skills?

3

STEP 3: IMPROVE THE ORGANISATION'S PERFORMANCE THROUGH COACHING

Leading and managing are two separate attitudes. Each delivers different results.

This chapter explores how you must use the skill of coaching to help your organisation establish a high standard of excellence. You will practise your skill of coaching and quickly synthesise critical information as you help your hypothetical friend, Brian, set the tone.

After reading this chapter, you should be able to

- take charge of setting the tone at the top of your organisation by addressing key weaknesses.

- provide and apply specific tools that will foster balanced risk-taking in your organisation.

- persuade other leaders to define and embody accountability so it becomes a cultural norm.

- enhance governance inside your organisation without the need to establish new or stronger policies.

The roles outlined in previous chapters may be new ways of thinking about yourself as a CFO, controller or other senior management accountant. Here are some titles that may help you begin to imagine yourself into these roles:

- Chief Strategic Officer

- Philosopher King of Finance

- Manager of Strategic Planning & Institutional Insight

- Chief Planning & Strategy Officer

- Orchestrator of Financial Management

- Accounting Strategy Leader

- Leader of Fiscal Discipline, Insight & Foresight

This book will use "CFO" to name this evolving position; you may find it useful or inspiring to employ one or more of the titles just listed.

CFO = INFLUENCER

An important role for the CFO is to influence his or her employer's culture for the better. This is not a responsibility you can opt out of.

Each employee with whom you come in contact, and many who simply hear about you, observe how you behave, which influences how they behave. Therefore, as a CFO, you should be well-versed in how a leader influences and even transforms an organisation's culture.

That is what you will learn in the following four best practices.

Exercise: Who Is Driving Your Train?

Instructions

Part 1: Think of five areas in which your firm regularly faces or takes risks or is vulnerable and list them in the table. Next, enter the name of the person who is responsible for managing the area at risk. Last, think about that person's individual approach to risk-taking using the following spectrum of attitudes.

SPECTRUM OF ATTITUDES TOWARD RISK-TAKING				
FLYING WITHOUT A NET				BLACK AND WHITE
Aggressive	Assertive	Middle of the Road	Conservative	Very Conservative

RISK AREA	PERSON MANAGING THIS RISK	PERSON'S ATTITUDE TOWARD RISK-TAKING
1.		
2.		
3.		
4.		
5.		

Part 2: Answer These Questions

What did you notice about the prevailing attitudes towards risk-taking in the people who are "driving the train" in your firm?

Is the attitude of the person managing your risk area appropriate, too much or inadequate?

Is there a balanced view towards risk-taking in your organisation?

Exercise: Brian—Part 2

Your task is to take the following two actions:

1. Read the following "Best Practices" information section. Use this information to devise ideas to help Brian arrive at solutions to his leadership challenges.

2. You have agreed to be Brian's coach so that he can be successful as a CFO. Read the "About Your Friend Brian" section.

Best Practices

Issue 1: Shape the Culture by Defining It

Main question:

What cultural structure should Brian put into place so that he can focus more on the big picture, yet know that necessary work will get done? What should his overall strategy be?

Specific questions:

What does Brian need to be aware of?

What specific tactics does Brian need to employ over the next year?

What will Brian need to measure to know that he is effective?

Refer to figure 3-1.

Issue 2: Create Balanced Risk-Taking by Establishing a Risk Programme

Main question:

How can Brian use a defined risk management programme to help this enterprise from throwing good money after bad ideas?

Specific questions:

What does Brian need to be aware of?

What specific tactics does Brian need to employ over the next year?

What will Brian need to measure to know that he is effective?

Refer to figures 3-2 through 3-6.

Issue 3: Foster Accountability by Defining It

Main question:

How can he influence Ruwan and Kimberley to pay close attention to their behaviours so that the firm can pull out of its death spiral?

Specific questions:

What does Brian need to be aware of?

What specific tactics does Brian need to employ over the next year?

What will Brian need to measure to know that he is effective?

Refer to figure 3-7.

Continued on p.44

Issue 4: Establish a Governance Programme That Weeds Out Questionable Practices

Main question:

> *How can Brian persuade Ruwan and Kimberley to buy into a governance programme for the entire enterprise so that there is less need for redundancies and controls?*

Specific questions:

> What does Brian need to be aware of?
>
> What specific tactics does Brian need to employ over the next year?
>
> What will Brian need to measure to know that he is effective?

About Your Friend Brian

Brian knows that stepping up as a leader and influencing the managing directors will help solve many of the long-term issues (issues 5 through 8), that R & K Enterprises faces. If Brian is proactive in setting the tone at the top of the organisation, many of these problems will become manageable.

He needs coaching on determining strategic priorities for the next 12 months.

Issue 5: Ruwan and Kimberley Practice Differing Standards

Certain managing directors and core employees are allowed to ignore internal controls because they are not obligated to report their actions to either Ruwan or Kimberley.

> ### Example 1
> In the landscaping business, the nephew is allowed to pocket cash when he gets busy and then wait until the end of the month to turn it in, to the extent that he remembers what it is. He also hand writes client invoices and sometimes forgets to make a copy. Brian is never sure of the business's actual revenue number.

> ### Example 2
> As vice president, Ruwan can sign company checks. He sometimes comes in on the weekends and gets into Brian's accounting system to issue checks to himself or another agent for expenses they have incurred or to reimburse a tenant. Securing documentation for these transactions is virtually impossible.

Issue 6: Ruwan and Kimberley Show Favouritism

Kimberley plays favourites when it comes to providing funding and setting goals—and whom she excuses for not meeting goals. Each managing director is required to submit an annual operating plan and goals for each year. Each month they meet face-to-face with Kimberley to go over the plan and goals. Brian has noticed that certain managers are regularly let off the hook when they overspend, do not reach their goal or mismanage resources. Most of these managing directors have either worked for R & K for more than 15 years, are members of one of the families or are long-time friends of Ruwan or Kimberley.

Issue 7: Ruwan and Kimberley Use Inappropriate Metrics

In three largest business units—retail, wholesale and manufacturing—Ruwan, Kimberley and the managing directors focus 100% on profits as their main measure of success. The reason for this, Brian surmises, is that these are the cash cows that feed the trust, fund the purchase of new businesses and cover the losses of the smaller units. The smaller units are measured and managed by operational nonfinancial metrics. These smaller units Brian refers to as the "pets."

Issue 8: Ruwan and Kimberley Do Not Practice Risk Management

Since they define themselves as owners of a "small business," neither Ruwan nor Kimberley believe in seeing the downside of anything. They are eternally optimistic and ignore any evidence that goes against this optimism. As a result, Brian is certain that the firm's insurance agency has placed them in very high-risk classifications.

Brian's Position Description (Important Elements)

Expected Results

Improve cash flows of the entire organisation by 10% the 1st year, 20% the 2nd year and 30% or more the 3rd year

Create an internal management reporting or scorecard system that provides timely information on each business entity and the entire organisation

Improve the internal controls of all entities and establish acceptable loss levels for each business unit

Develop a risk management programme for the entire enterprise in order to reduce insurance costs by at least 25%

Improve the quality and speed of the annual planning process

BEST PRACTICE: SHAPE THE CULTURE BY DEFINING IT

Over time, people are conditioned to mimic the leaders they follow.

Tone at the Top

Throughout human history, stories have been shared about great leaders and what made them great. We speak about George Washington's humility, Oskar Schindler's compassion, Confucius' frugality, Stephen Hawking's vision, Mohandas Gandhi's courage, and Eva Perón's passion.

As a leader, you must tell a story to your followers. It is about them, not you.

The Leader as Proactive Shaper of Culture

The story you tell is the culture you shape around your team and organisation. You cannot help but tell this story because a culture is always a reflection of the leader's attitudes, behaviours and beliefs.

As proof, take the following test.

Exercise: Your Team's Story

Instructions

Check all those words that your customers would use to describe your team.

	Customer-focused		Difficult to do business with
	Private		Open and transparent
	Fun		Serious
	Careless		Careful
	Trustworthy		Devious
	Disorganised		Organised
	Precise		Close is good enough
	Risk averse		Risk taking
	Creative		Old fashioned
	Inconsiderate		Respectful
	Technology friendly		Technology phobic

Answer Key

Whatever descriptions you selected, if you are the leader of this group, these traits also describe you.

CFO Tool: Cultural Ideals

The organisation's culture can be a leader's best tool for establishing and carrying out a specific intention.

Five Culture Principles

1. An unmanaged culture never gets better, it only gets worse.

2. The culture of a team or organisation is a direct reflection of its leader.

3. Your organisation's culture determines the effectiveness or ineffectiveness of your team.

4. When employees do things that are detrimental to your success, it is the symptom of a major problem. These people are being rewarded for their actions.

5. A leader cannot ask or force people to adopt the organisation's values. The employees either have similar personal values, or they do not. Only those who have similar values will live up to the organisation's values.

Culture Defined

Culture is instinctive. Any time two or three people join to work together on something, they create a culture. Culture is the mood, attitude and atmosphere of an organisation. It has an effect on almost every result.

Another way to define culture is to understand "How things get done around here." You will understand your organisation's culture by discovering answers to the following questions:

- How is change handled?
- How are employees rewarded and for what?
- How is poor or faulty communication handled?
- How are new ideas dealt with?
- How is dishonesty dealt with?
- How are the goals set?
- How are goals achieved?
- How hard will employees push to achieve their individual goals?
- How do the leaders deal with managers who don't follow the rules?
- How are managers who make ethical decisions recognised?

The answers to questions such as these—the truth, not necessarily what you want to hear—will tell you a great deal about your operational dynamics. Operational dynamics refers to how people communicate, cooperate and coordinate. It is a fundamental way of producing the innovation and fresh ideas needed to keep a business strong and healthy. Understanding what works to help or hinder operational dynamics is a key to leading with intention.

Connect the Dots

Every decision, behaviour and action has an effect on something in your organisation. You know this; however, most of the time the impact of these actions is undiscovered or ignored.

If you intend to foster a healthy culture, you must connect the dots for others so they understand the mechanisms of cause and effect. It is almost impossible to isolate the individual cultural component or process that contributes to poor decisions or inappropriate behaviour. Still, an understanding of the norms of your culture will give you information about what employees consider important and their attitudes.

Your corporate culture can be either your ally or your downfall in being a great CFO.

The Story You Tell

If your employees are performing activities not related to the organisation's values or mission, you must determine why.

As a leader you should pay attention to your organisation's story, which extends beyond the walls of your building. Employees share the story, not only with each other, but also with customers, prospects, vendors, lenders and the general public. Accordingly, you should examine and consider changing your existing story.

If your current story or culture is one of ethical, caring, productive, challenged and contributing employees, not much change will be required. However, if you are like the majority of employers, your story is one of dissension, silos, information hoarding, miscommunication, clueless leaders, unproductive workers, weak accountability and poor decision making.

If any of these descriptors sound familiar, you should activate this leadership responsibility. If the work your employees transact does not further the organisation's mission or purpose, the reason is embedded in your story.

Ingredients of a Culture

What you may not know about culture—even though you probably have a good intuitive sense of what it is—is that culture is made up of 10 unique pieces. These 10 pieces fit together like a mosaic, and each one affects the other. They all must be in place for the mosaic to exist, and they must create a cohesive picture or image to be useful.

Your Culture Mosaic

Figure 3-1 is an image showing how the 10 unique mosaic pieces fit together. The centrepiece of all culture mosaics is the leader's attitudes, behaviours and beliefs. This leader can be an individual, team or family, which is why this is the most important element of each mosaic. Your culture can hide or expose poor decisions, fraud, waste, conflicts and silos.

Figure 3-1: Culture Mosaic

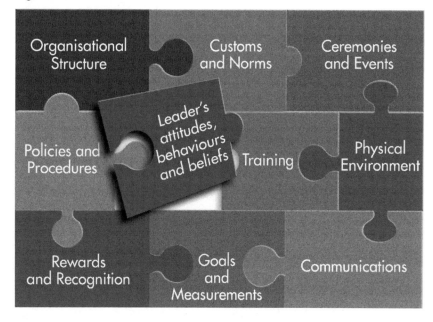

The Cultural Mosaic Components:

- Organisational Structure
- Customs and Norms
- Ceremonies and Events
- Policies and Procedures
- Leader's Attitudes, Behaviours and Beliefs
- Training
- Physical Environment
- Rewards and Recognition
- Goals and Measurements
- Communications

People are often influenced by stories more than by facts and figures.

Each story you tell as a leader must be on target.

This brief summary gave you a basic understanding of culture so you can address your cultural norms regarding how employees face up to their responsibilities. The following case study will illustrate how components of the mosaic fit together in this case, creating a negative situation that led to the company's visible and painful downfall. Here is a recent one.

Exercise: Washington Mutual's Demise

The Starting Point—The Fatal Decisions

In 2003, Washington Mutual (WAMU) adopted a corporate slogan of "The Power of Yes." Around the same time the leaders decided to heavily rely on adjustable rate mortgages (ARMs) because of Wall Street's ravenous appetite for them and because the accounting rules of revenue recognition allowed them to book all the revenue up front without needing to be concerned, in terms of profit, about the risk of bad debts.

Leader's Attitude, Behaviours and Beliefs (Tone at the Top)

Kerry Killinger, CEO of WAMU, had a vision. He wanted his institution to be the biggest provider of financing for the American public. He envisioned WAMU being among the top five retail banks. He made acquisitions, one after the other, that helped him fulfil that dream. Some were risky, but he felt the risks were worth it because of his charter to do so as stated in the organisation's vision and mission.

WAMU's Vision

"Becoming the nation's leading retailer of financial services for consumers and small businesses."

WAMU's Mission

"Building strong, profitable relationships across a broad spectrum of consumers and businesses. We will do this by delivering products and services that offer great value and friendly service, and by adhering to our core values of being fair, caring, human, dynamic, and driven."

WAMU's Values (As Extracted From its Entire Statement)

"We are never satisfied with the status quo and know that we must continually reinvent our organisation and ourselves."

"We continuously drive operational excellence to innovate our products, processes, and services."

"We are committed to excellence and the achievement of superior long-term returns for our shareholders."

"We set high, measurable goals and hold ourselves accountable to achieve them."

Organisational Structure

With each acquisition it became more difficult to both control and maintain the desired culture consistently, despite their worthy values. Experienced management was spread thin due to the challenges that came with WAMU's meteoric growth as it went from a one-state institution to a national entity with branches or offices in all 50 states. Branches were opening faster than a fast food chain.

With each acquired bank, more of the branch and office managers were permitted to pursue their own directions as long as they met their goals and performance metrics.

Goals and Measurements

The primary measurements that Killinger and his direct reports used to define success were the following:

Share value

Quantity of loans sold to Wall Street

Balance of loans outstanding

Revenue (when the "Power of Yes" became the mantra, WAMU's revenue went from $707 million in 2002 to $2 billion in 2003)

Growth (from 1996 to 2002, WAMU grew to become the nation's sixth largest bank)

Continued on p.50

Notice they were not measuring the quality of those mortgages and credit card balances. This is because the accounting rules allowed WAMU and other institutions to recognise the deferred interest on ARMs as income without booking any bad debt provision, even though they were on the hook for bad loans. ARMs commanded higher fees than conventional mortgages. When Chase took over WAMU's portfolio, it estimated that 82% of the ARMs were impaired, as were 15% of the credit card balances outstanding.

The week prior to WAMU's implosion, Kerry Killinger was bragging to an audience in Seattle about how well the bank was doing.

Customs and Norms

At WAMU, the "Power of Yes" gave employees the tacit approval to make a loan regardless of whether the applicant qualified. The pressure to produce loans came from senior management. Everyone's job became "getting the job done" (that is, bring in and approve loans while steering applicants to ARMs). Employees' workloads made it impossible to perform quality reviews, check credit scores, verify income and, ultimately, determine if applicants could pay back the loan. WAMU employees had on average, only 35 minutes available per loan file.

As a loan processor, if you said "no," the loan application was removed from your desk and given to an employee who would say "yes." Employees who turned down an applicant were either written up or terminated.

Policies and Procedures

To perform a proper valuation of a residential property, competent appraisal firms generally require about 40 hours. This was not satisfactory for WAMU because it slowed down its loan process. In 2005, a policy change allowed employees engage appraisers who could complete the process faster and cheaper. This led to appraisal work being done by unqualified appraisers who never actually visited the property and often relied on websites to evaluate the property's worth. If a lower-quality home, on the same block, was worth $300K, while a group of higher-quality homes on the same block were worth $600K, the better homes were used as comparables in determining the value of the property being appraised.

To keep the pipeline of resalable mortgages filled, WAMU lowered qualification standards, especially for those who needed ARMs. If the applicant was alive, the loan would be granted. The policy as extolled by supervisors was, "It is not your job to worry if the customer can pay. Your job is to write the loan."

The policy on loan application files became, "A thin file is a good file."

Rewards and Recognition

WAMU paid incentives as high as $10,000 in the form of commissions to agents who brought in applicants and to brokers who steered them to mortgages that WAMU could package and sell.

WAMU's underwriting employees were urged to fund the mortgage, while the top producers were lavished with rewards and incentives. One high-pressure mortgage centre in Southern California produced $1 billion in loans just in 2004. The team's leader was lavished with bonuses, along with being a perennial member of Kerry's President's Club and receiving multiple awards at the Club's annual meeting. Other mortgage centre managers wanted to receive the same recognition.

The Ending Point—Lack of Accountability via Denial and Blame

Kerry Killinger to this day refuses to accept any culpability for his role in the demise of WAMU and the harm suffered by thousands of homeowners, investors and employees. Despite pocketing $103 million and refusing to pay back a dime of it, and despite telling the U.S. Congress that he took "full responsibility" for the bank's failure, Killinger also claimed, "I'm certainly very disappointed to think about my customers [borrowers] lying to me. But that's fraud, and it shouldn't happen."

Sources: *The Seattle Times, The Seattle Post Intelligencer, Seattle Metropolitan Magazine, Business Week, Wall Street Journal.*

In the End

The good leader builds high morale and creates community in their team and organisation.

Knowing your firm's culture and how it works will enable you and other leaders to become better leaders. You, when setting the tone for the culture, must understand how the culture you formed affects your efforts to produce results and fulfil the mission. Your culture is not formed by policies and words alone. It is a complex and dynamic mosaic that must be shaped by managing through the 10 mosaic pieces as part of your leadership intention.

Exercise: Does Your Organisation Have These Weaknesses?

Instructions

Place a check by each of the following if you have seen examples of it within your organisation.

YES	I SEE THIS HAPPENING WITHIN THE ORGANISATION:
_____	Conflict regarding important strategies, goals or policies
_____	Adversarial conditions or silos in specific departments, groups or professions
_____	Information stockpiling or dishonesty by certain individuals
_____	Communication errors that go without being addressed or frequent communication errors
_____	Leaders who do not heed advice, listen to their employees or follow the rules
_____	Unproductive workers, especially people who are permitted to do low quality work or waste time
_____	Low level of accountability toward commitments being fulfilled or low level of accountability with the organisation's customers and other stakeholders
_____	Poor decision making that is not addressed, corrected or improved

Answer Key

For each item you checked, you have a damaged story. These problem areas will arise occasionally, but when they become the norm, your culture mosaic has weaknesses in various components. These will negatively affect any goals set or improvements a leader contemplates.

CFO Lesson

Culture trumps policy 100% of the time.

BEST PRACTICE: CREATE BALANCED RISK-TAKING WITH A RISK PROGRAMME

Proper risk management is determining the cost you cannot afford before you take the risk.

Exercise: Self-Test

Part 1: Answer These Questions

Do you take risks?

How do you know that you do or do not take risks?

Is it because other people tell you that you do or do not?

Is your answer because of your definition of risk?

Part 2: Check Those Activities That You Define as Risky

	I CONSIDER THIS TO BE RISKY FOR ME TO DO:
_____	Driving a race car at more than 200 miles an hour
_____	Flying commercially once a week
_____	Mountaineering
_____	Deep sea fishing
_____	Driving fast on a busy road
_____	Having children
_____	Pursuing a university education

Risk Is Individual to Each of Us

Each of these activities will be considered risky by some and not risky by others. For example, many people may consider having a child or 2 not to be risky, but may find 5 or 10 children more risk than they can tolerate. And then there are people for whom the thought of having even 1 child is just too risky. Likewise, a university education can carry a high cost in both money and effort, and at the same time choosing the wrong field of study can lead to underemployment or unemployment.

Your daily trips to and from work may carry a greater risk than you driving on a race track at 200 miles per hour. But which of these activities do you consider more risky?

Diverse Spectrum of Attitudes Toward Risk-Taking

Consider risk taking on the individual level as a range across a spectrum going from "black and white" on one end to "flying without a net" on the other. How you value something will determine where you place yourself on the spectrum. You could be black and white about your finances but fly without a net when it comes to your job. You are not at one place on this spectrum for everything you value, nor do you stay in the same place all your life.

Five Risk Management Principles

1. The negative impact of risk-taking is greatly reduced when you analyse the real cause of the undesirable results.

2. Because you cannot control all risks, it is much healthier to be prepared for the worst and expect the best.

3. People do not take risks because of fear.

4. Risk-taking is a necessity for individual and business success in this changing world.

5. What we define as risky is all about the specific value we assign to the "thing" that we place in jeopardy.

The Value of What Is At Risk

As the firm's CFO you must help define the value of both the tangible and intangible things that are put at risk each day. These include

- reputation,
- brand,
- future,
- income stream,
- sustainability, and
- integrity.

Risk Is Everywhere and Never-Ending

The best place for the CFO to add value to his or her employer's risk management programme is to help the organisation to define its operational risk appetite.

Operational Risk Defined

Operational risk management looks at the business from the operation itself and is defined as the risk of direct or indirect loss resulting from inadequate internal control, processes, people and systems to react to external events. Financial information is not enough to gauge a company's overall business risk.

The value of managing operational risk is only slowly gaining recognition. One reason is that by the time the financial impact of management's misjudgement affects the balance sheet or income statement, it typically is too late to do anything about it other than pick up the pieces. By tracking operational indicators and metrics, leaders can identify opportunities and threats before they affect the company's finances.

One approach to measuring operational risk requires firms to routinely review many nonfinancial factors such as the quality of corporate governance, employee morale, customer satisfaction, implementation of goals and execution of those goals, the company's application of technology, and its deployment of those practices. Numerous tools that enable you to easily measure operational risk already exist, such as the balanced scorecard, activity-based costing or driver-based forecasting.

Why Defining Risk Is Necessary

CFOs prove their worth when they assist their firm's leader in defining, measuring and monitoring the risks that could be costly or disastrous.

Answer These Questions:

How does your organisation define risk?

What is a risky activity or decision and what is not?

How do you and others know?

The Meaning of Risk Has Changed

Boards of directors and other stakeholders of corporations are becoming more wary of risk. To ensure their own job security, CEOs must be more aware of the need to develop sophisticated means to measure and manage everyday business risks. Numerous experts agree that there is less tolerance by stakeholders, especially in public organisations, for executives who do not prepare for a disaster of some sort. This leaves boards, shareholders and executives searching for broader and better ways to manage risk in order to achieve their goals and ensure strategy viability. Thus, the entire organisation must focus on the causes of risk instead of the traditional method of only treating the symptoms or focusing on protection through insurance.

Operational risk management is managing the risk of loss resulting from any of the following:

- Inadequate processes or systems
- Human factors
- External events

Operational risk management requires defining *authority* and *accountability* for each sort of identified risk.

In your organisation, like all others, the answer to the question of whether an activity is risky often varies. For example, if you are a start-up company in your first years of existence and your funding is shaky, your definition of acceptable risk is going to be very limited. The opposite could also be true. Because you have little to lose, it may be acceptable to throw caution to the wind. Many successful firms started out this way, like Apple Computer and Microsoft.

If your organisation is well established and has survived at least 15 years, the definition of risk will be much broader and wider. Your leaders may decide that growing by 150% in one year is too risky, but growing incrementally at 30% per year is an acceptable risk.

What if your company is a multi-billion dollar international conglomerate? Your leaders' definition of risk is going to be extremely different than the start-up's definition.

From 2007 through today, much of the world has faced a major economic downturn and restructuring of the global banking system. In this painful recession, the majority of our companies operated conservatively, cut expenses and strove to weather the storm, yet a large number of organisations used this difficult period as an opportunity to go on merger or acquisition sprees, to spend more on research and development, to invest in new products or new customers, or to create new channels. Risk is always in the eye of the beholder.

Fundamental Sources of All Business Risks

In managing risk, it is of vital importance for the CFO to be aware of the most basic sources of risk. You show yourself to be a great leader when you spend time examining these sources to look for problems and opportunities, because good governance requires the finance team to do this in real-time.

Source No. 1—Your Firm's Business Model

Strategic planning is managing change and overcoming risks. Strategic planning is a process through which risk can be identified in advance and dealt with proactively. See figure 3-2 for an example of the strategic planning flowchart.

Figure 3-2: Strategic Planning Flowchart

Strategic planning starts with your mission statement because it sets the organisation on a course and instigates change from today's status quo to where you want to be in the future.

The second element of strategic planning is your actual strategic plan, the measurement of your mission. In this document you identify specific metrics and methods of measuring whether you are accomplishing your mission over the next 18–24 months.

Information from the strategic plan flows into the operating plan, which identifies the technology, facilities and people you need to achieve each specific objective in your strategic plan. The operating plan is where you are headed and what you will commit to accomplishing in the next 12 months.

Out of your operating plan comes your financing plan. In this document you highlight the methods of payment for the technology, facilities and people in your operating plan. For instance, how much capital will come from internal sources and profits? Will some of the funds come from outside investors? Will additional funding be required from banks or other lenders? Your financing plan will address these questions.

Finally, from the financing plan, you develop your budgets: the operating budget, the capital budget and the balance sheet budget. These three documents become your control and feedback systems over the risks and changes that you started with your mission and strategy. An overview of a risk management programme is outlined in figure 3-3.

Figure 3-3: Proper Risk Management Programme

Your global risk management programme consists of your operating plan, financing plan and the three budgets (see figure 3-3). What goes badly wrong in many organisations today is that the leaders see risk management as a function of insurance. This job is assigned to a senior management accountant or a risk manager, a position that today many firms have outsourced or eliminated. The risk manager is rarely included in the strategic planning process. This means that your executives embark on a global plan, ignoring risks or underestimating their cost, and then turn the risk analysis over to the senior management accountant or risk manager. They drop it on that person's desk and ask, "Do we have adequate insurance coverage for this particular risk?"

This is a fatal blunder.

As you can see from the strategic planning flowchart, the risk management programme must be a main agenda item of strategic planning done offsite when the leaders decide the next year's plans. This is also the time they define what risk is. Good and effective risk management, like governance, requires a team approach. An effective programme consists of a cross-functional team of people throughout the organisation who examine risk holistically.

Source No. 2—The Mindset of the Risk-Taking Entrepreneur

Whether it's a defensive reaction or simple optimism, most business owners refuse to contemplate the possibility of failure. It is as if the word does not exist in their vocabulary. This attitude can be ruinous, wasteful and costly; hurt people; and spoil opportunities for future success. Most entrepreneurs see themselves as the types of people who put their heads down and charge full steam ahead. However, you can badly injure yourself with that mindset. This person does not avoid risk, but ignores it at every opportunity. This person does not recognise that failure is an option. This is why risk can be mismanaged or unacknowledged.

In understanding the possibility of failure in risk-taking, there is a very delicate line to walk. It is better to assume failure can occur than to resign yourself to it. It is acceptable to acknowledge our fear but not let ourselves be overcome by it. Walking that line requires courage.

Source No. 3—The Mindset of the Risk-Averse Person

Though many people prize and value those who take risks, there are groups of people who tend to be risk averse. Risk avoidance comes from two human concerns: (1) all people hate to lose money, and (2) all people hate to look incompetent. People in management accounting own the mentality, "I am the guardian of the assets," and this attitude often leads us to look at risk differently than anyone else.

When you make a critical decision on taking a risk, your decision is composed of the following:

- How emotional versus. how rational you are

- How confident versus how anxious you are

- How impulsive versus how reflective you are

Risk is inherent in almost everything that a business does, including expansion, mergers, research or contraction. Therefore, no matter how much a decision is researched, a typical management accountant must understand the fact that uncertainty will always exist in any strategy and decision.

As CFO, you want to make sure that you do not do anything irresponsible. But that is very different from taking a risk. Your job is to put forth the best alternative, suggest the pros and cons, identify the opportunities that we seek, and then show what the future could look like in both scenarios. While evaluating this risky situation, we must watch for potential gains or upsides as well as potential losses or costs.

Management Accounting Sits in the Middle as a Fulcrum

Management accountants, especially as controllers or CFOs, are a fulcrum of the organisation. They are in the midst of a delicate high-wire act and must make sure that they manage this balance very carefully. They cannot afford to push the organisation too far on one side. If they solely focus on the controls and checks and balances or are perfectionists about people crossing all the T's and dotting the I's, they foster a culture in which no one is willing to take any risk. History is littered with businesses that were unable to out-innovate their competitors or keep up with the evolving marketplace.

On the other side of the balancing act, we have employees and leaders who want to be innovative, strive to be creative, and push the envelope on innovation, ideas and processes. Our job is to support them and not let them undermine the success of the organisation.

CFO Solutions to Make People Aware That Risk Exists

Solution 1—Wisdom Sharing

Share best practices across your organisation. For this sharing to occur, your culture must be one of openness, with managers as interdependent partners within the risk environment. This partnership must include employees from the operational side of the business and employees whose advice is often ignored such as the audit, finance, human resource and risk management teams.

Solution 2—Governance Structure

Implement a governance structure. This is an integral part of the firm's operational risk programme. Governance promotes cultural transparency and openness together with demanding accountability from each employee, each operating unit and every support function.

Solution 3—Measuring What Is Important

Identify, collect and monitor a balanced set of critical performance indicators or metrics that help the leaders to identify control issues and allow for early mitigation. This solution is also important to operational risk management.

CFO Solutions to Make People Aware That Risk Can Be Survived

Solution 4—Knowing What Is Risky and Why

Unless an employee can quickly identify why something is risky, they will not become aware of alternatives to pursue until it is too late. Provide each employee with this next tool and teach them how to use it before they leap into the unknown.

CFO Tool: Risk Identification

This is a two-part tool using questions and a flow chart that will help you, as a leader, look at risk differently. Part one of the tool is six very important questions that need to be asked before a risk is undertaken. Part two is called the critical risk path. Walking this path step-by-step before the organisation takes a major risk will help leaders and others make more intelligent decisions.

Part One—Addressing Tough Questions

Figure 3-4 outlines six critical questions associated with determining risk.

Figure 3-4: Critical Risk Questions

What is the worst that can happen?

What is the best that can happen?

What is the most likely outcome?

What are the negative effects of the likely outcome?

How can we handle the negative effects?

How will we minimise or protect ourselves against the negative effects?

Part Two—Defining the Critical Risk Path

Once you have determined a risk's likelihood (see critical risk path diagram figure 3-5), you move to the choices you have in addressing the risk. One option is to accept it. Another option is to minimise it. There are plenty of actions to take before undertaking the risk to keep its impact or cost low. A third option is to insure, but that does not mean that insurance is your only option. Sharing the risk, such as partnering with another firm or putting a stop-loss through a limited investment of both time and money, is a way to insure the risk.

Figure 3-5: Critical Risk Path

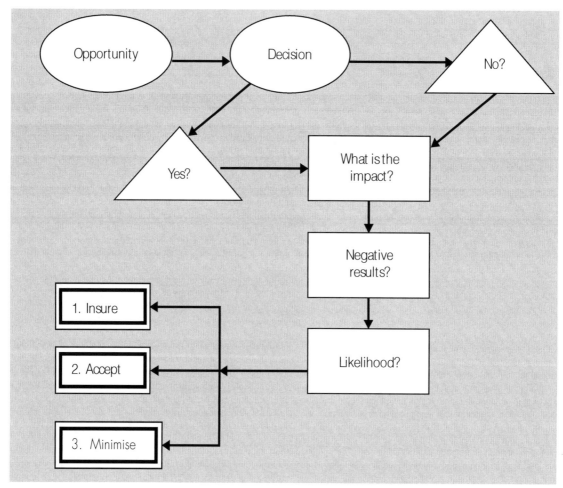

Best of all, your three options are not mutually exclusive. For example, you could accept part of the risk, insure part of it and closely manage it so that you minimise the potential downsides.

Solution 5—Knowing How to Manage a Risk

Once the risk has been identified and employees understand that they need to address it now, not later, they will need guidance on how to react. Provide all employees with this next tool and train them how to use it so they can become aware of each risk and its impact.

CFO Tool: Selecting the Right Strategy

Figure 3-6 helps you to quantify risk based on two variables—likelihood and negative impact.

Figure 3-6: Risk Strategy Grid

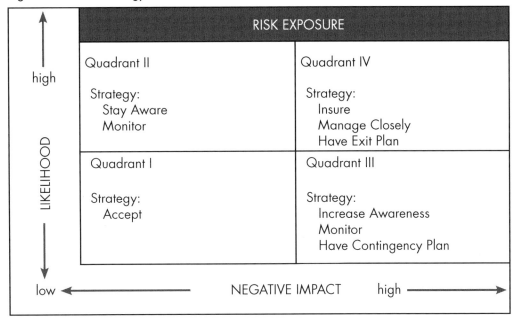

This risk strategy grid is a matrix that is often used to assist decision makers to foster smarter decisions. It applies to everyday risk management as well.

Not having an exit plan can have negative effects. Some organisations continue to dig themselves into a deeper hole in that the leaders refuse to believe that failure can happen. The belief that "failure is not an option" worked fine for the first space voyagers, but very few shareholders exist who support executives who throw good money at bad opportunities. There were a lot of dotcom executives whose only business model was to set up a company, and then have an IPO so they could cash out as millionaires. When their business model proved to be worthless, they did not have alternatives lined up.

In the End

Organisations that incorporate proper risk management into their daily operating strategy achieve better returns and help to stabilise their earnings. By employing this best practice and the tight controls built into it, your company avoids the pain of people who colour too far outside the lines or who underestimate the cost of a specific risk.

To avoid any negative outcome and promote shareholder confidence, the organisation's leaders must instil transparency regarding the risks that the organisation is undertaking; especially those that will build but also harm shareholder value. Incorporating risk management into your culture will result in leaders being able to trust and empower employees more.

Exercise: Do We Manage Risk Well?

Instructions

Complete this self-test to see if you are adequately managing the everyday risks that your organisation faces. Place a checkmark next to the questions that you answer with a definite "Yes." Compare the total number of boxes you checked with the answer key at the end.

_____ Am I able to sleep at night without worrying about risk in my organisation?

_____ Do I have a clear understanding of firm-wide risk, the organisation's key areas of vulnerability, and our ability to recover quickly?

_____ Am I confident that an accountable executive is addressing each risk, large and small?

_____ Is there a process or function within my organisation that is responsible for assessing, measuring and monitoring risk?

_____ Have we created a realistic balance between innovation and protection?

_____ Do our cultural norms help us ensure that all costly risk is identified before we take it?

_____ Does my organisation have an operational system or process for evaluating risk?

_____ Do I have complete assurance that financial and operational controls are being used as designed?

_____ Does a thorough and appropriate reporting mechanism exist that allows for an adequate checks and balances system for sparking fresh ideas, fraud prevention and managing risk?

_____ Do I have assurance that financial and other information is reported correctly?

_____ Are our processes for risk assessment, management control and governance evaluated and reviewed for both efficiency and effectiveness on an ongoing basis?

_____ Is there an emphasis and supporting process within my organisation for aiding productivity and for improving operations?

_____ Are my organisation's stakeholders provided with reliable assurances that their investment is protected by ethical and sustainable means?

_____ If I were not part of the organisation, would I be comfortable with the assurances provided to me as an outside stakeholder or investor?

_____ Do we have a specific written recovery plan in the event that we suffer as a result of a major risk?

Answer Key

13–15 checked—Congratulations!

You have a high Risk IQ. Keep doing what you are doing and improve those areas you did not check off.

10–12 checked—Good job

You are effectively managing your risk but are still vulnerable in many areas. Get started on removing those weaknesses today.

7–9 checked—Scammers love you

You have many areas of vulnerability. Start addressing them immediately.

0–6 checked—Sharpen your resume or CV

Your company may be out of business soon.

BEST PRACTICE: FOSTER ACCOUNTABILITY BY DEFINING IT

It is impractical, even impossible, to hold an employee to a standard that is never defined for them.

Accountability From a Leader's Perspective

Fostering accountability is a skill that all leaders and most management accountants need to be better at. You can easily and significantly influence accountability when you understand it at a deeper level.

Exercise: Are You Accountable?

Everyone in your department is talking about a story, usually a rumour, about what the CEO did over the weekend.

What is the proper course of action?

Choose:

_____1.   Listen to the rumour and share the story with others.

_____2.   Urge your coworkers to stop listening to and spreading the rumour.

_____3.   Ignore the rumour.

_____4.   Tell the boss about the rumour being spread.

_____5.   (Enter your own choice)

In what ways are you accountable in this situation?

In every situation you have a choice. Accountability is enhanced when you make the responsible choice based upon high standards and a commitment to being good. Much of the time, we don't think about our choices and their impact, and our accountability weakens.

Accountability Is Often Misunderstood

Many people talk about the need for accountability but often cannot define it. Instead, we assume that we and others know what accountability means.

What Is Accountability?

Following are three realities about accountability.

- *Accountability Reality 1*—In order to effect accountability in others, we have to take an honest look at ourselves and understand how others see us.

- *Accountability Reality 2*—Issues of accountability are all around us. It is important that we become aware of them.

- *Accountability Reality 3*—Many people think they are accountable. They are most likely being responsible, but as they define it.

To further understand accountability, review these important principles.

Five Accountability Principles

1. Everyone is born without an understanding of accountability. We learn it from the people around us. If they have it, we learn it. If they lack it, we do not learn how to be accountable.

2. When we are accountable, we own all our obligations and duties. We don't rent them.

3. The level of accountability in your organisation is an indicator. Lack of accountability indicates that your organisation has weaknesses or does not support accountable behaviours.

4. Strengthening accountability starts by examining our own actions and attitudes. If we are not changing for the better, we are changing for the worse.

5. Strengthening accountability starts with you.

Accountability Defined

Accountability is keeping your word, meeting your commitments and taking full ownership for your actions. Accountability is accepting reality without finding fault, placing blame or hiding from the truth.

The most important aspect of accountability is standards. When you clearly set a standard for someone to live up to and he or she meets or exceeds that standard, then that person is accountable. When the person does not meet that standard, despite having the ability to do so, that person is not being accountable. Therefore, when you do not live up to your own standards as defined by your values, then you are not being accountable to yourself.

True leaders hold themselves accountable.

Everyone Is Involved in Instilling Accountability

An entire group of people is necessary to help hold someone accountable. This applies at all levels: family, team, company, community and society. At its very essence, accountability means accounting for one's own actions. Whenever you say that you want someone to be accountable, in effect you are saying, "I expect you to account to me for the action you took or the decision you made."

Where Accountability Fits In

To better understand how these individual pieces fit together, review figure 3-7, the accountability target.

Figure 3-7: Accountability Target

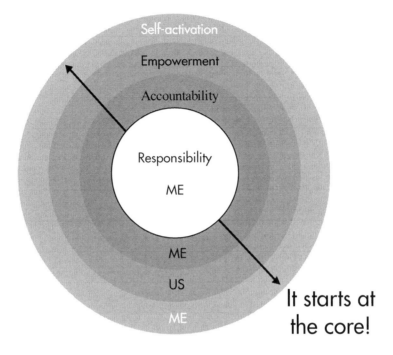

Leaders of organisations desire employees who think for themselves and are self-motivated. To achieve this goal, it is important to first look at the centre of the target. At the core, the team member chooses to be or not to be responsible. This person takes responsibility for his or her actions, decisions and behaviours. Like an apple, if the core is rotten, the apple is of no value to anyone. Similarly, if the employee takes no personal responsibility, you will be unable to develop a self-activated employee.

From the centre we go to the next ring, accountability. This is where the leader expects employees to be accountable for their actions and behaviours and support the team and the team's decisions.

From accountability we go to the next ring, empowerment. This is the level where the leader creates a team or organisation culture that tells the employees they have the freedom and flexibility to take matters into their own hands, with certain limitations. Employees know that they will be held accountable for their actions and decisions but also know that you will support them should they make an error in judgement.

At the outermost ring of the target is a level of self-activation. Employees understand that they have been empowered and use this mantle of authority to look for things that are not currently being done, or intercede when there is a vacuum of leadership. One of the hallmarks of "employer of choice" organisations is that leaders emerge whenever they are needed. Organisations create self-activated employees because they are empowered, accountable, and, most important, take personal responsibility seriously.

If the core is missing, you will never foster accountability, empowerment or self-activation.

The Undefined Standard

You tell your employee: "Fatima, I want you to be more accountable." Fatima's automatic response is: "Accountable to what?" Your face-saving answer is: "You know what I mean."

The sad fact is that Fatima does not know what you mean.

As you saw in the previously discussed principles, learning what accountability means starts in your childhood, and its context is defined by your parents and other adults in your life. Therefore, if you have 200 employees in your organisation and you say globally: "I want you all to be more accountable," these 200 individuals will default to their own definition unless someone has proactively and clearly defined accountability.

It is a duty and obligation for your organisation's leaders to establish what accountability means as it fits into your organisation's cultural ideals.

Enhancement Requires a Common Definition

As you read earlier, enhancing or strengthening accountability within an organisation starts by establishing realistic standards, with great expectations, for employees at every level. High levels of accountable behaviours are a direct result of four ingredients.

1. The expectation for each person to behave in an accountable manner is embedded as a cultural norm.
2. A unanimously accepted definition of what accountable behaviour looks like within and without the organisation.
3. A methodology for holding each person to those standards and weeding out those employees who do not live up to this expectation.
4. A screening process that determines if a prospective employee can and will buy into this cultural norm.

Before delving into leaders' and influencers' role in strengthening accountability, take a look at why it is beneficial to embed accountability into your organisation's ongoing story.

Why Accountability Works to Make Everyone Successful

While it may seem obvious that accountability helps to build a successful team and company, it may be useful to review a few of accountability's most important benefits. High levels of accountability

- establish individual integrity.
- contribute to corporate integrity.
- ensure employees follow through on their commitments.
- guarantee people can rely on the team and one another.
- allow team leaders to spend less time acting as their employees' supervisor.
- build employees who are dependable, yet can act independently.
- remind employees to hold themselves and each other accountable.

How Leaders Improve Accountability

Because accountability is something that is affected by what leaders do and say, it is very important for leaders to take the first step and model accountable behaviour. This section provides a few specific suggestions of things that a CFO or controller, as team leader and executive, can do to show that he or she takes accountability seriously. By modelling these behaviours, these leaders communicate the expectation that grants them the permission to hold others accountable.

These three suggestions are explained in the following sections.

1. Monitor Your Own Actions

- Meet all your own commitments.
- Be consistent in your words and actions.
- Catch people doing things right.
- Identify and remove barriers to honesty.
- Be open to new ideas.

As a leader, you must be very self-aware of each thing that you do and say. Leaders are very visible, and employees take their cue about acceptable behaviours from them. For example, if you refuse to engage in blaming others but instead immediately move to resolution, you show others that this is the accepted norm. If you support every policy, even the ones that affect you negatively, you model that everyone needs to support the organisation's policies.

2. Use Honesty

- Instil and value honesty in others.
- Accept differing opinions and views.
- Seek solutions instead of blame.
- Give timely and honest feedback.

You must always tell the truth. Of course, there will be information that employees do not need to know or must be withheld for legal or strategic purposes. Even in these cases, however, you must always strive to tell the employees the truth. This does not give you permission to be blunt and rude. Leaders use tact when being honest. By being honest and expecting honesty back from others, you set the expectation that you value the truth. One thing that almost every human being on this planet despises is a negative surprise. Honesty helps to decrease the likelihood of that occurring.

3. Hold People's Feet to the Fire

- Give employees authority with responsibility.
- Require employees to meet their commitments.
- Do not accept excuses for less than full efforts.
- Set measurable targets with each employee.
- Let employees know exactly what you expect from them.
- Do not use excuses for your errors and mistakes—own up to them.

> **Example**
>
> If you request the XTZ report from Herman by Friday, do not allow him to come to you Friday morning and say, "Is it OK if I get the XTZ report to you Monday afternoon? I have been very busy and haven't gotten to it yet." The team leader who wants to be popular will say, "Herman, that's OK. I know you've been busy." By doing so, the leader undermines the team's accountability by not enforcing expectations of timeliness and real-time communication, especially if this is the first time you were aware that Herman was unable to meet the deadline to which he agreed.

10½ Rules of Accountability

1. Issues of accountability are all around us. The starting point is awareness.

2. Without a common, understood and accepted definition of accountability, I will never be able to effect any change to it.

3. Accountability is a nebulous concept until we define what it means for us. It is like quality—"I know it when I see it." A common definition gives us a basis for understanding and communicating.

4. In order to encourage accountability in others, I have to take an honest look at myself first and understand how others see me and my actions.

5. Before I can do anything about my organisation's accountability, I must open my eyes to the level of accountability my team demonstrates in our daily actions and decisions.

6. Improving accountability in others begins when I choose to be accountable each day.

7. Once I decide to question another person's accountability, I automatically give them permission to question my accountability.

8. When we find fault with each other, we decrease accountability. Focusing on the problem or issue without placing blame will help us to create solutions more quickly.

9. If we focus on what is not working and place blame for things that go wrong, we won't move forward in enhancing accountability.

10. We become immersed in our culture and soon lose sight of its make-up. It is critical to step back and regularly reexamine our organisation's cultural ideals to see if they are building or hurting accountable behaviours and decisions.

10½. Strengthening accountability starts with me.

Exercise: Self-Test: Are You Accountable?

Instructions

Part 1: Rate yourself on a scale of one to seven for each item to determine if you demonstrate accountability with your actions. Do not guess; be brutally honest and see yourself through the eyes of those you work for and with.

This is how well I show integrity. My family or best friend would say

I forget to walk my talk.		I usually walk my talk.			My actions and words agree.	
1	2	3	4	5	6	7

This is how well I take responsibility for my actions. My family or best friend would say

I ignore my responsibilities.		I am normally responsible.			Everyone can count on me.	
1	2	3	4	5	6	7

This is how I take ownership of my results. My family or best friend would say

I don't like what I have.		What I have is okay.			I accept everything I have.	
1	2	3	4	5	6	7

This is how often I place blame or find fault. My family or best friend would say

I say, "I never make a mistake."		I sometimes blame others.			I never blame others or find fault.	
1	2	3	4	5	6	7

This is how I feel about my future. My family or best friend would say

I dread what comes my way.		I often create my own luck.			I create everything that happens to me.	
1	2	3	4	5	6	7

Answer Key:

If most of your responses are 6 or 7 you might be in denial about your commitment to being accountable. At times you will play the victim or feel like blaming others because you are human. Being in denial is the first sign of someone who lacks accountability.

If most of your responses are 1 or 2, you are being too hard on yourself and could benefit from a more objective view.

If your responses were 3, 4 or 5, you understand what accountability looks like and are self-aware about your behaviours.

Part 2: Answer This Question

How accountable are you? How well do you demonstrate to others your commitment to being accountable?

BEST PRACTICE: ESTABLISH A GOVERNANCE PROGRAMME THAT ELIMINATES QUESTIONABLE PRACTICES

Weak governance is self-perpetuating and self-expanding.

Quiz

What is governance?

_____	A book of our policies and code of conduct
_____	Our system of controls
_____	A system of checks and balances
_____	Having a police chief
_____	Something our code of ethics addresses
_____	All of these
_____	None of these

Correct Answer:

All of these and none of these. This is not a trick. By the end of the section you will understand why both of these answers are correct.

Controls or Policies Are Not Governance

Today, the following are expectations placed on the management accounting profession:

- The public expects us to prevent fraud.
- Our employer expects us to increase the bottom-line.
- Oversight agencies expect us to ensure transparency.
- Boards of directors expect us to provide better governance.

At the same time, a small group of individuals have tarnished this profession's reputation because of illegal and unethical acts.

Society demands transparency from the CEO. So the CEO and the board look to their finance group to create the infrastructure of governance.

Governance Defined

Governance is a high level governing philosophy; thus, an organisation's leadership body has a primary responsibility to guide, direct and shape how its organisation is operated and led. Governance is not a policy manual, list of procedures, code of conduct or system of internal controls. In fact, it is not any specific written document.

Governance is

- a philosophy,
- a commitment, and
- a promise.

The organisation's leadership body defines for its shareholders, vendors, customers, employees, the public and themselves how it intends to protect the trust placed with it. It promises to follow this definition and back up all promises with a commitment to play "the game" fairly.

The Game of Business

Because the leadership team is the body that establishes the tone, sets the rules and decides how to keep score, it controls the game. Governance is a public communication about how the leadership team will ensure the game is honest and fair. No one wants to be involved in a game that is rigged and the outcome fixed in advance.

Your organisation's stockholders are placing their bets on your organisation that they have a fair chance to win, that is, they will be rewarded for putting their money on the line and investing it in you. Therefore, anything that your organisation does to harm the stakeholder's trust communicates: "We don't honour the trust you placed with us." Organisations that do not practice good governance tell stakeholders, "We need you but we don't care about you. We are more important to our success than you are."

Today's Organisation Is Complex

An organisation is made up of the following:

- Tangible assets
- Capital
- Technology
- Buildings and facilities
- Debt
- People
- Intangible assets such as
  - ideas,
  - energy,
  - brand,
  - reputation, and
  - potential

- Processes and systems
- Communications
- Promises

And much more.

Notice that some of these items are measurable and many are not.

Best and Highest Use
This is why governance is a philosophy. When your leadership team establishes governance, it decides how to best use all these resources to accomplish the organisation's mission.

Makeup of a Governance Programme

Governance is built around the organisation's mission or purpose. That is always the first component. The next component of governance is corporate values. Values are the selection and publication of the behaviours that make the mission achievable.

Core Value Defined
A core value is a highly prized trait or quality that, in an organisation, defines how its mission will be fulfilled. The mission sets your people on a journey. Your core values explain how you and others on this journey must behave.

Example—Core Value of Honesty

"We will grow to become the best in our industry by being honest with everyone inside and outside the company."

Your founders' promise and commitment is that being honest will pay off in numerous ways. Anyone— vendor, customer, employee or shareholder—who cannot be honest is not invited to join you.

Corporate Culture's Role
The third component of governance is culture, which is also known as "the tone" and is made up of 10 mosaic components.

In proper governance culture is important because

- your firm's culture impacts almost every result from profits to accountability, ethics to risk taking.
- your firm's culture brings forth success or failure with equal efficiency.

Culture is covered in the first best practice in this chapter.

Morale Is Vital in Governance
Recently, a consultant in the human resources field cited several U.S.-based surveys that found more than 80% of employees are unhappy at work because they do not like their jobs or employer, and they are actively looking for something else. Similarly, 82% of executives are currently looking for new jobs.

Answer These Questions:

Assume that one of your executives is searching for a new job.

Is this employee likely to be concerned about the success of your organisation?

Is this employee looking out for your company's best interest?

Assume that your best employee is unhappy and cannot wait to leave.

Would he or she likely be concerned with controls?

Culture Must Never Be Downplayed

Culture is important because it exposes governance breakdowns rather than hiding them.

The Culture Statement

This is the tool used to define the desired culture. Chapter 4, "Step 4: Improve Your Team's Effectiveness Through Coaching," discusses this important governance tool.

Furthering the Makeup of a Governance Programme

After the mission, values and culture statement, the governance programme extends the overriding philosophy to

- processes,
- policies,
- strategies,
- plans,
- goals, and
- relationships.

The final component is your system of controls—operational, financial and external. All components are put into place to ensure that everyone in the organisation behaves themselves and lives up to the philosophy your leaders have established.

Following are graphical and metaphorical explorations of governance.

The Active Atom

Like a useful yet volatile atom, your firm's governing philosophy must harness and employ the energy of items that manage the enterprise, while preventing the atom from turning into chaos.

The Human Element in Governance

People are the unknown factor of managing and leading as it relates to governance.

Governance Controls this Unknown Factor

People pursue their own self-interest. When their self-interest is in agreement or alignment with their employer's, they will follow the philosophy. When an employee's self-interest does not coincide with the employer's, the governance programme must help the leaders discover this lack of alignment so they can deal with it.

Cost of Governance

By now, you may be thinking that the governance programme is an expensive and time-consuming endeavour and that only large organisations can afford to have one. If you think this, you are incorrect. Remember, governance is a philosophy.

In small and medium-sized organisations, establishing the governance programme is easy, provided it is done properly. You can have a good governance programme without incurring a high cost. The cost is putting all the elements of your active atom containment system in place and then monitoring them ensure that they propagate the leaders' governing philosophy.

Exercise: Does My Organisation Know Governance?

Instructions

Complete this self-test to see if your organisation currently has adequate governance.

Check "Yes" only if you can answer with 95% assurance that this occurs in your organisation.

Check "No" if you are unsure or know that this is not taking place.

QUESTIONS TO ANSWER	YES	NO
Have our executives taken the time to implement a governance programme in our organisation?		
Have our executives established clear expectations about the ethical standards of how we do business?		
Do we have a proactive board of directors that holds executives accountable to doing what they say they will do?		
Are employees who don't follow policy or break the rules called to task timely and appropriately?		
Does our executive body define for everyone the cultural norms it desires and then demonstrate these in its daily actions? Examples include honesty, openness, trust and ownership of results.		
Totals		

Answer Key

If you answered "Yes" less than four times, then your organisation does not have a viable governance programme.

Because governance is an area in which the finance function plays a major role, it affects your entire team's effectiveness as well as your ability to rely on the system of internal controls.

4

STEP 4: IMPROVE YOUR TEAM'S EFFECTIVENESS THROUGH COACHING

A leader's primary responsibility is to create an environment in which our employees can successfully complete their work.

One area in which CFOs and controllers must enhance their skills is in developing a strong and supportive team. In this step, we explore five best practices that enable the CFO to build a such a team. Each practice is one dimension of the overall theme of teaming. Today, CEOs highly value controllers and CFOs who have the ability to develop a cohesive team around them.

After reading this chapter, you should be able to

- employ specific tools that turn a department into a real team.
- apply specific strategies that foster individual accountability.
- evaluate if your recognition efforts support behaviours that create collaboration.
- use feedback to build star performers.
- help employees be more effective so you can lead better.

THE VALUE OF TEAMING IN FINANCE

Teaming is the way that work gets done today.

Like it or not, our work has become a series of projects. Closing the month-end is a project. Getting ready for the audit is a project. Implementing the new cost system is a project. The controller and CFO who sees the accounting function as a series of projects can easily apply the concept of teaming as a way of getting the work done more effectively, while enhancing employees' productivity. Because the accounting department really is an information business, the best way to get work done smoothly requires employees to be able to easily communicate to one another and arrive at decisions quickly. Teaming, as an operating style, uses consensus as a way of making decisions that benefit everyone.

No longer can the head of accounting be the type of person who sits in the office oblivious to what is going on outside the door. The CFO is an equal and participating member of his or her team. Not understanding this imperative will be detrimental to your career because CEOs value the manager who is a dedicated team builder. If your CEO sees that you lack the ability to build and lead a strong team, he or she will quickly replace you with someone who can.

Here are two more realities of being the leader of the finance team to keep in mind as we explore these four best practices.

- *Reality No. 1*—The success and failure of any team ultimately is dependent on the quality of its leadership.
- *Reality No. 2*—Leadership is more about the people you lead than it is about you. If you do not know how to lead, you will be unable to tap into and bring forth the full potential of your team.

The CFO as Developer of Team's Skills and Talents

A person who achieves results as a leader of a small team will supersede the leader without results who is leading hundreds. Whether you are a leader-manager or a leader-executive, you need people. This is why every leader must strive to foster interdependence.

However, you will never create an attitude of interdependence until each team member and you fully become accountable, which leads to reliability and competence.

Exercise: Is This Your Management Accounting Team?

I enter your management accounting department with a problem. You are at your desk, and I present you with my tale of woe.

Which of these answers will I get from you?

1. ____ "That's not my area. Come back when Lin is around."

2. ____ "Send an e-mail to Lin when you get back to your desk. If I remember, I will tell her you stopped by."

3. ____ "I will have Lin call you."

4. ____ "Give that to me. I will make sure it gets resolved and one of us will get back to you no later than tomorrow morning."

If you checked "4" you have an understanding of interdependence and you act in ways conducive to a capable CFO.

However, do not congratulate yourself yet. Here are two key questions to answer.

Does everyone on your team practice interdependence?

Would each individual on your team provide me with answer 4?

In Essence

Accounting is a team concept and not an independent function. The work needs to get done regardless of who does it. As CFO, you must build an interdependent team whose sole focus is to satisfy the needs of every one of management accounting's customers.

Remind your team often of the following:

No matter how important you are, remember that an organisation does not depend on the efforts of any one person.

Exercise: Brian—Part 3

Your task is to take the following two actions:

1. Read the following information about best practice areas.

2. Read the section "About Your Friend Brian," who needs your assistance so he can be successful as a CFO.

Best Practices

1. Shape Your Employees' Teaming Behaviours with a Solid Structure

Main question:

What cultural structure will Brian need in place so that he can focus more on the big picture, yet know that things will get done? What should his overall strategy be?

Specific questions:

What does Brian need to be aware of?

What specific tactics should Brian employ over the next year?

What will Brian need to measure to know that he is effective?

Refer to figures 4-1 and 4-2.

2. Shape Your Employees' Accountability by Establishing Behaviour Expectations

Main question:

What sorts of standards must Brian instil so that his team delivers quality, timeliness and confidentiality? What should his overall strategy be?

Specific questions:

What does Brian need to be aware of?

What specific tactics should Brian employ over the next year?

What will Brian need to measure to know that he is effective?

Refer to figures 4-4 and 4-5.

3. Shape Your Employees' Behaviour by Using Honest Feedback

Main question:

How can Brian use frequent feedback to change or improve employees' behaviours? What should his overall strategy be?

Specific questions:

What does Brian need to be aware of?

What specific tactics should Brian employ over the next year?

What will Brian need to measure to know that he is effective?

Continued on p.78

4. Shape Your Employees' Behaviour with Recognition and Rewards

Main question:

What sorts of behaviours does Brian need to recognise and reward and what could the rewards look like? What should his overall strategy be?

Specific questions:

> What does Brian need to be aware of?
>
> What specific tactics should Brian employ over the next year?
>
> What will Brian need to measure to know that he is effective?

About Your Friend Brian

Brian is still working through his challenges with his employer, R & K Enterprises. It is now time to face up to those people who Brian relies on if he is to be more effective in his existing role.

The following single issue contributes to Brian's inability to delegate many of his responsibilities to other employees.

Issue 9: Employees Lack Professionalism

R & K is situated in a small community, so there are few well-paying jobs except for those with the businesses that R & K owns. Despite this fact, several of the management accounting employees act like Brian or R & K owes them something. Many individuals treat coworkers with disdain. Another group has a hard time getting to work on time or lets their personal lives take precedence over their work obligations.

Even though the shared-services concept was launched long before Brian was hired, the employees in each discipline have yet to commit to this structure. Most define themselves by their specialty and many silos have formed within the department.

The members of the shared-services group physically located in the business units use the excuse "Corporate is making me do this" whenever they must enforce a policy. They blame Brian whenever they do something that upsets their managing director, which is quite often.

All R & K employees not in management, except for Brian's team, receive regular semi-annual performance evaluations. HR felt that the new controller should take this project on.

BEST PRACTICE: SHAPE YOUR EMPLOYEES' TEAMING BEHAVIOURS WITH A SOLID STRUCTURE

"Never doubt that a small group of thoughtful, committed people can change the world. Indeed is it the only thing that has."

—Margaret Mead

The Teaming Culture

Your goal is to foster a team, as esteemed researcher Margaret Mead describes, that can be counted on to change the world with the work they perform. As the trends in chapter 7, "Step 6½: Improve by Making a Commitment," demonstrate, you likely have fewer resources available to you to get the job done in a timely and productive manner. This is why you must work to develop a teaming culture within your department. The teaming culture is one in which every member is a fully participating peer who has equal say in the decisions and whose contribution is valued. A team is more than just a group of people who have been thrown together in a room or set of cubicles. The team, to be successful, must be made up of members who own these two attitudes:

- If the team is to succeed, I must do everything in my power to make that happen.

- If I fail to deliver, then the team suffers and I let down my team.

In the teaming culture the team is only as strong as the weakest performer. Therefore, a true team works together to raise the performance of every member, so there are no substandard performers.

Interdependence Defined

Television and movie versions of *Star Trek* have always fascinated me because of their characters. In every version of this visionary franchise, the characters struggle to figure out how to work and function interdependently. Despite the fact that each character has a role (for instance, captain, engineer, officer or ensign), they realise they cannot survive the rigours of space without cooperation with one another and coverage for the person in distress.

As the leader of the finance team, you have many tools available to foster and support a teaming culture of interdependence. A CFO always implements the following three tools first.

Team Vision

Your team's vision is a definable destination that your group strives to reach sometime in the future. You, as the leader, set the vision that flows from the entire organisation's vision. If any incongruence exists between the team's and the organisation's vision, you will have difficulties in determining which of the two takes priority.

Team Mission

Your team's mission is an uplifting, inspiring statement about who your group is and why it exists. Again, you as the leader take the lead on developing the team's mission, but you also include the input and ideas of team members. For them to buy into the mission and support it, each member needs to feel that his or her input helped to determine what the team is all about.

Study samples of actual team missions as outlined in figure 4-1. They will serve as examples in developing a mission for your own team. Some are humourous, which helps to energise members.

Figure 4-1: Examples of Team Visions and Missions

"We strive to be the only blameless group when things go wrong."

"We create new perceptions of what is possible."

"We want to be recognised as the best management accounting unit in the region by our customers and by our firm's leaders."

"We will become the leading and quoted authority on the topic of ethical accounting procedures in the country."

"Our daily intent is to become the most innovative, reliable solution maker in the entire organisation."

"We believe that human beings inherently are worthy of our respect, and we practise this in our daily interactions."

"We are dedicated to being the best at bringing people together to solve financial problems."

"We are in the business to help our internal customers achieve their operational and financial goals."

"Our mission is to provide outstanding service to each and every client – internal and external."

"We keep the lights on."

"We catch other people's errors."

Team Structure

As explained previously in this section, you do not create a team by putting a bunch of people together and declaring, "We are now a team." The group must have a structure to help support behaviours that foster a teaming culture. The following items are often neglected or overlooked when a group, such as management accounting, attempts to evolve from a department to a team:

- Rewards for high quality service and for behaviours benefiting teaming and professionalism
- Rewards that recognise individual contribution
- Rewards that recognise the entire team for their combined efforts
- Penalties and consequences for behaviours detrimental to teaming and professionalism
- Communications systems
- Work-tracking methodology
- Attendance requirements (if you regularly have work and staff meetings)
- Meeting formats (if you regularly have work and staff meetings)
- Agendas (if you regularly have work and staff meetings)
- Standards for behaviour (for instance, ground rules)
- Participation requirements and standards
- Planning ahead methodology
- Ways to have fun

Diversity

In order to succeed in the long term, the team must be able to accommodate and handle diversity in a professional manner. This type of diversity has nothing to do with heritage; it has to do with differences in how each person perceives the world. The team will mature as it discovers how to incorporate the diversity of the following items, while capitalising on those differences when it comes to making decisions, setting goals and rewarding itself. Team success requires diverse

1. opinions,
2. experiences, and
3. personalities.

The Team's Decisions Are Made by Consensus

To have a true team culture, all major decisions must be made by consensus. This is difficult to do given the nature of the person who is attracted to management accounting and the diversity previously described. Nevertheless, creating a team culture in which consensus is honoured, valued and used is relatively easy once you understand what it is and how it works.

There is tremendous misunderstanding about what consensus is, because we all have participated in groups that attempted to build consensus and were not able to. Let us start by reviewing definitions of consensus. The first is the most difficult to instil in people because it means that when you are on a team, you must let go of your individual ego.

Team Consensus Defined

Consensus is an acknowledgement that the team is more valuable that the individual.

Consensus is the process of everyone sharing their thoughts before deciding. Consensus is getting everyone's input and concerns. Consensus is making a decision that will move the team ahead. When it comes to creating consensus, the most critical aspect is to proactively get every person's concerns and feelings on the table long before the decision is made. What often undermines consensus is that the people involved in the decision were not heard or their opinion was not valued. Then the person becomes distressed and is unable to support the decision. When you do take into serious consideration everyone's opinion, no matter how difficult or challenging, you will arrive at a decision that everyone can support, even if it goes against what someone wants.

Consensus is fully supporting each team decision 110%.

The last part of the definition of consensus is the most critical to building a team culture. This means that after the decision is made no member of the team can downgrade its importance. Because this degree of support for a decision is rare, some managers and executives do not believe in consensus. What universally happens is that a decision that affects many people is made by a few without the input of those affected. This is a pitfall you want to avoid.

As before, let us examine the polar opposite definition. Consensus is not any of the following:

- 100% agreement
- Agreement by majority vote

- Imposed by the leader

- Impossible

More Characteristics of Consensus

As the consensus spectrum in figure 4-2 illustrates, consensus is not making decisions by dictum or directive. It is also not making decisions by majority rule. And consensus is not 100% agreement. On the decision spectrum, consensus is between making decisions by majority rule and 100% agreement. In every major decision, at least one person will disagree or believe another way of solving the problem exists.

Figure 4-2: Consensus Spectrum

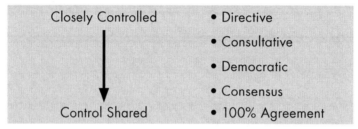

The goal of consensus is to enable the team members who disagree to buy into the solution or decision by incorporating their ideas and concerns. In doing so, the outcome is one that they can support because it addresses what they are most concerned about.

Another pitfall to avoid when seeking consensus is the situation in which the leader has already made up his or her mind, lets the team discuss the issue, and then makes the final decision he or she wanted all along. This is not only a waste of time, it is something that many of us have experienced in the past and has added to our mistrust of consensus.

Questions the leader asks of the team before it decides will enable team members to support the final decision or outcome.

- *"How will the customer be best served?"*

- *"Will this action or decision move us toward our goal?"*

- *"What can everyone agree to?"*

- *"If we don't act or decide, what will likely happen?"*

Teams use consensus to decide on important issues such as the following:

- Resolving conflict

- Format for meetings

- Consequences for not living up to the team's standards

- Rewards

- Communication methods

- Tracking work and the progress made towards team and individual goals

- Attendance requirements at meetings

- Acceptable participation levels
- Process for getting honest input that will lead to consensus

How to Create a Strong Team

Time and patience are the two most important ingredients that the CFO puts into the mix in order to create a strong team. The group of employees that you wish to become a real team needs time to practise their teaming skills. It is very difficult to let go of our individual identity so that we can work on a collective one.

Along with time, you need to give your team members lots of room to make mistakes as they learn how to work together as one unit. This is when patience comes in. The following are the hallmarks of a team that works well together. Notice that they use the specific tools mentioned earlier, such as a shared vision and a common mission.

Characteristics of an Interdependent Management Accounting Team

- Shared vision
- Clear mission
- Recognition of one another's contributions
- Clearly defined roles
- Mutual accountability
- Team-based rewards
- An attitude of "We win together or we lose together but we choose to win."

Eight Team Principles

1. For your team to share your vision, it must be compelling and exciting to them.
2. A shared vision ensures that we are moving toward the same ultimate destination.
3. To communicate your mission, you must be able to define it yourself and for each team member.
4. Making employees feel important creates a strong, loyal team.
5. A clear mission enables employees to believe in the value of their work.
6. To create a clear mission, everyone in your group should feel involved in creating it.
7. An uplifting mission carries us through times of confusion.
8. The team is only as strong as the weakest member.

10½ Rules About Building Effective Teams

1. Teams are shaped, not delegated.
2. Team attitude is developed, not dictated.
3. Your customer does not care about titles, rules, responsibilities or hierarchy.
4. Customers want their needs met.
5. Customers see a department or team as one unit.

6. The more mistakes the team makes, the faster it learns to do it right.

7. Teams need specific milestones to measure their progress to work as one.

8. Whenever a team member delivers bad service, this act poorly reflects upon the entire team.

9. Whenever a team member delivers good service, this act reflects well on the person, not the team—unless this member gives specific credit to the team.

10. The team leader's purpose is to replace himself or herself by giving every member the opportunity to serve as the team's leader.

10½. A team is only as strong as its weakest member.

There are two additional best practices that interdependent teams rely on to be effective and cohesive:

- Culture statement
- Behaviour standards

In the End

To all of management accounting's customers, each of you is an interchangeable part.

The controller or CFO who wishes to build a cohesive group that supports each another and function as one unit without the need to be closely managed must look to the process of team-building to enable the group to work as one. Teams can be successfully developed if you facilitate the group in creating their own tools, structure, value system and the standards that help them to foster their own team culture.

Exercise: Signs of Interdependence in Management Accounting

Now envision the work you perform as seen through the eyes of your customer. Customers do not distinguish between an AP specialist and a GL clerk. They know that an employee works in management accounting and that they need this team to solve their problem. You can easily verify if a team has an attitude of interdependence by the following hallmarks. Whenever a group truly is interdependent, every employee on the team adopts the following attitudes and models the related behaviour.

Instructions

Only check "yes" for a trait if everyone you serve would say your team exhibits it regularly.

TRAIT OR ATTITUDE	WOULD OUR CUSTOMERS SAY THIS IS TRUE FOR MY TEAM?		
EACH DAY...	YES	NO	UNSURE
Every one of us can and will help any customer.			
We cover for the person who is out.			
We trust each other.			
We know we can rely on each other.			
Every goal is our goal.			
Everyone's priority is the team's priority.			
We regularly share what everyone one is working on.			

TRAIT OR ATTITUDE	WOULD OUR CUSTOMERS SAY THIS IS TRUE FOR MY TEAM?		
EACH DAY...	YES	NO	UNSURE
We assist the person who has more work than time.			
Even when the leader is out, we make decisions and make things happen.			
We share resources and ideas.			
We strengthen the weakest link on the team.			
We never cover up our mistakes.			
We focus on solutions rather than on blame.			
We hold one another accountable to the standards.			
We share the credit for our success.			
We win together or we lose together, but we choose winning.			

Answer Key

13–16 "yes" responses: You have a great team.

Less than 13 "yes" responses: You have some work to do. Pay close attention to the tools in this chapter.

CFO Lesson

You cannot lead a group to be a real team unless you create the path.

BEST PRACTICE: SHAPE YOUR EMPLOYEES' ACCOUNTABILITY BY ESTABLISHING BEHAVIOUR EXPECTATIONS

When your employees know how to act because you have made it clear to them, they will make their own decisions without asking permission and direction.

Expectations and Standards Shape Behaviours

Behaviours that are measured get attention. Once you determine the culture and behaviours you want and expect, you must be able to honour them. Clear expectations in the form of team ground rules and a culture statement are excellent tools to define the standards for employee behaviour. Rules about work reinforce the values identified in your culture statement.

The most important step in the learning curve of people figuring out how to work as a team is how well they enforce holding each other accountable. This is when the leader sets the tone for the rest of the team by encouraging each member to be watchful when someone does break a ground rule or standard and immediately lets the person know. Standards only work well when the offenders understand that they will be immediately notified about failing to adhere to one.

Example—Dress Code

Your company's dress code sets forth a standard that, if not adhered to, will be lowered in a short period of time. Typically, a company establishes a dress code to enforce an expected standard of behaviour regarding the clothes that employees are allowed to wear.

The reason that employees do not adhere to this code is because the following frequently happens.

The first time an employee dresses in a manner that is not in line with the code, either no one notices or nothing is said to the employee. Another employee, emboldened by seeing someone else getting away with, for example, more casual clothes, will follow suit. Other employees notice and they too will dress in what they define as appropriate or feel comfortable wearing.

Later, when somebody with authority notices the drastic decline in professional dress, the employee who is most inappropriately dressed that day is called out. The employee then says, "But this is been going on for months and no one said anything. Look at Nicolas over there. He is dressed worse than I am, so why are you picking on me?"

By this time it is almost too late to do anything without causing tremendous dissension and consternation about what is appropriate and what is not. The result is that the official dress code is abandoned and the standards lowered.

The first time an employee violates a standard, this behaviour must be challenged that day. Each other time someone else is inappropriately dressed, you must remind them as well. If the clothing item is not addressed by your code, you must immediately update the code and announce the change. Most importantly, if there is any stated penalty for being inappropriately dressed—being sent home to change or losing a day's pay—that penalty must be enforced in each situation, regardless of person or reason.

Unless these actions take place timely, over time the overall standard of dress will rapidly deteriorate and you will be unable to return back to the original standard.

More Accountability Principles

1. Leadership and teamwork go hand in hand. One is fully dependent on the other.

2. The great leader creates the environment in which his or her followers can win too.

3. Employees always model their leaders' behaviours.

Power of Expectations

When you provide and communicate a clear, high expectation to someone, the person will almost always rise to the occasion. The reason that employees are not accountable is that their leaders do not communicate what they expect of them. To be accountable you need to know what you are accountable to and responsible for. Whenever you ask an employee to live up to a standard that only you know about, you have manipulated, not led.

One reason that an employee fails to meet a standard is that you have set the bar too high or too low. A second reason is that you have not made the standard clear, have not provided the reason for it or are not living the standard.

Your Role in Fostering Accountability

It Starts on Their First Day

The day you clearly communicate the standards that will make your team and each member succeed starts their first day on the job or on your team. You can jump-start a commitment to accountability when you explain your expectations during the interview process.

Suppose a job candidate discovers that he or she must be accountable and live up to high expectations in order to be part of the team. If the candidate lacks this attitude and commitment, he or she will often screen himself out. Once the employee is on the team, constant reminders about the team' high standards will ensure those behaviours get written into the script about which actions are appropriate.

Cultural Objectivity

When an employee has become part of the culture story, it is hard for him or her to be objective about it. When you become inured to your own culture, you no longer notice those actions that undermine mutual accountability.

Principle of Inculturalisation

Every organisation experiences the Principle of Inculturalisation.

Nothing is more frustrating for a supervisor than having employees who are focused on their paycheck, not their responsibilities. If employees are focused on "what's in it for me" in terms of their paycheck and benefits, they will not have sufficient time left to satisfy their customer, internal or external. Yet, what many leaders do not realise is that they create this situation.

Inculturalisation Defined

Inculturalisation is the point when the employee becomes indoctrinated into the culture and loses objectivity. It is the transition time when the employees are now part of the story, playing their role in fulfilling it.

What Employees Expect Today

What employees desire, more than a paycheck, is an employer that practises supportive cultural norms so that employees

- are clearly supported by their supervisor.

- receive recognition for their efforts.

- receive regular coaching on where they stand and what they can do to improve their performance.

- are allowed to be involved and have a voice in their goals and the team's direction.

- are granted empowerment and freedom to do their job as they see fit.

- see that accountability standards are enforced upon everyone.

- receive feedback on their performance.

In other words, loyal, contributing and caring employees demand to be treated as human beings and not machines or disposable items.

Inculturalising Starts on Their First Day

On day one, when an employee is hired, their main measurement of worth to you and your commitment to the employee becomes his or her paycheck and benefits. As time passes, the employee's attention naturally turns toward his or her responsibilities.

Then, at a specific foreseeable point in time, the employee becomes part of the culture and his or her attitude may change.

Point of No Return

The CFO wants employees to focus on their responsibilities and services to their customers. If cultural norms do not provide the supportive environment that today's employees demand, they will develop a mercenary attitude and use their paycheck as a measurement of their worth and your commitment to their success. Once this point is reached in your work relationship, it is almost impossible to change the employee's attitude. Despite the hundreds of management books written each year on how to reverse the rise and trend of this mercenary attitude, employees rarely alter their focus from their paycheck back to their responsibilities, even after the culture norms improve.

Leaders' and Supervisors' Contribution

As a leader and supervisor, you create the environment and write the story your employees enact each day. Therefore, you control whether or not employees develop a mercenary attitude.

CFO Tool: Culture Statement

The best way to develop a behaviour standard by declaring your culture story is at a team retreat. People can brainstorm the types of ideas they believe will enable the team to effectively work together and hold each other accountable. If your employees help create the culture story, they will buy into it willingly.

Figure 4-3 lists the defined culture story that Success Unlimited's finance team adopted years ago.

Figure 4-3: Success Unlimited Management Accounting Teams' Culture Statement

The employees of the Success Unlimited shared-services team support and enhance a culture that respects and practises these norms: We value...

- Respect for each other
- Openness to new ideas and innovations
- Open communication
- Demonstrated honesty and integrity in our actions, decisions and words
- Trust
- Privacy and confidentiality
- Flexibility
- Superior customer service
- Accountability
- Commitment to quality and accuracy

CFO Tool: Ground Rules

Just as in developing a culture statement, the optimal way to develop a behaviour standard is at a team retreat. People can brainstorm the types of ground rules or standards that will enable the team to effectively work together and hold each other accountable. Start the process by focusing on specific behaviours that are undermine team members' effectiveness. Then ask "What rule will prevent this behaviour from taking place?" Turn their responses into a specific ground rule.

Figure 4-4 lists the ground rules that Success Unlimited's accounting team adopted years ago and holds each other accountable to.

Figure 4-4: Success Unlimited Finance Team Ground Rules or Standards

- Honesty is requested and valued.
- Everyone equally participates in serving our various customers.
- Everyone is each other's equal and peer.
- Cooperation is expected.
- Show courtesy to others and we will be courteous to you.
- We will meet all deadlines.
- Invest your down time in growing your skills.
- What is discussed within the team stays confidential unless the entire team grants specific permission for you to share it.
- Expect honest feedback often.
- If someone breaks a ground rule or standard of conduct, she expects to be informed immediately.

CFO Tool: Service Standards

The customer service standard statement is a powerful tool that enables the CFO to help employees understand what is expected of them as they take on new challenges and responsibilities. Organisations that are committed to providing high quality service have one for the teams that provide service to the external customer. This definition helps to ensure that the employees adopt an attitude of service.

What works well externally also works well internally.

By working with your team and establishing 5–10 service standards, you can develop one that guides employees' contributions each day. Figure 4-5 provides Success Unlimited's customer service standards that guide the actions and behaviours of its management accounting team.

Figure 4-5: Success Unlimited Customer Service Standards for Finance

- Do the little things that help our customers do their job well.

- Maintain a sense of urgency about meeting your customer's needs.

- Work with customers to ensure they have defined their expectation about how and what they want, and when they want it.

- If you are ever uncertain, get immediate guidance before deciding.

- Set expectations with customers who are affected by a change in your priorities and keep them, your team and your supervisor informed.

- Use these specific prioritisation criteria for establishing the most important task or what to do next.
  - Providing meaningful or insightful information to your customer.
  - Taking care of the customers who cannot do their jobs and need your support.
  - Directing the customer to the right resource.
  - Improving anything that impairs your or someone else's productivity.
  - Preventing—permanently—bad information from entering the system.
  - Closing the month on time.
  - Fixing something that is broken instead of working around it.

In the End

"People are not your most important asset. The right people are."

—Jim Collins, *Good to Great*

It is the leader's job to clearly communicate what he or she wants from each employee in terms of commitments and behaviours. All too often, CFOs and controllers only address the measurable behaviours around the technical work they do, and they fail to address the soft attitudes that can undermine all other efforts.

As CFO, you can swiftly influence your team and others outside the team to behave in certain appropriate ways. Accountability can only be enhanced when the standard and expectations are made clear to every employee, all employees buy into them, and deviations from the standards are addressed swiftly.

You now have three specific tools to use that strengthen the team's accountability almost immediately.

Exercise: How Well Do You Clarify Expectations?

Instructions

Imagine yourself as you go through your workday and truthfully answer how frequently you perform these types of leadership activities.

DO YOU:	EVERYDAY	OFTEN	SOMETIMES	RARELY
1. Clarify each person's role and how it fits into the big picture?				
2. Address any employee's inappropriate behaviour immediately?				
3. Compliment or support positive behaviours immediately?				
4. Support those employees who do things appropriately?				
5. Enable employees to solve their own problems?				
6. Take a colleague to task who acts in an unaccountable manner?				
7. Check with others to determine if you are seen as reliable and accountable?				
8. Set clear expectations for how everyone on your team must behave, including yourself?				
9. Address the problem whenever someone does not live up to those expectations immediately?				

Answer Key

If most of your responses are not in the "every day" or "often" columns, then you are not helping to embed accountability into your team's DNA. It takes a lot of courage and awareness to address those instances in which an employee does not to live up to defined expectations and standards.

If most of your responses were in the "sometimes" or "rarely" columns then you need to step up and perform these actions more often. Each time you do not address an inappropriate behaviour or support a positive one, you weaken the fabric of accountability both in your team and your organisation.

BEST PRACTICE: SHAPE YOUR EMPLOYEES' BEHAVIOUR BY USING HONEST FEEDBACK

Power of Immediate Feedback

In order to ensure that an employee or colleague behaves in ways that are supportive, you must work on establishing specific consequences whenever a person, even you, does not live up to expectations or disobeys a policy.

Two Consequence Principles

1. A person's behaviour is determined by the consequences that immediately follow any particular behaviour.

2. Immediate feedback is a powerful consequence.

The most powerful way to alter a person's behaviour is through immediate consequence in the form of feedback. The longer the space between the behaviour and the feedback, the less likely the employee will change. Feedback that immediately arrives after the behaviour greatly increases the likelihood the behaviour will be altered or reinforced.

Delaying to address, condoning or ignoring a behaviour are consequences that reward an employee's behaviour. With an underperformer, each time you choose to delay, condone or ignore the behaviour you are rewarding that behaviour.

Alternatively, if an employee behaves in a way that you want to change, you must immediately call it to the attention of the employee and do so as soon as you notice it. You will see employees gain awareness of specific actions and change his or her behaviour for the better.

What Feedback Is and Is Not

Feedback is the truth about an employee as his or her manager sees it. From the employee's point of view, feedback means the difference between being in the dark and knowing where he or she stands. Feedback allows employees to see if they are who they believe themself to be. It provides employees with tangible information on how they are doing. Feedback is the favourite tool of successful coaches and leaders because it creates two-way dialogue with employees.

If feedback is driven by fear, employees will avoid it, anxious that you will punish them. To be an effective coach, you must build the habit of giving feedback when the employee does things right. The CFO all too frequently ignores positive actions and decisions and gives feedback only when the employee errs. Feedback is not criticism. Criticism is exactly what you give when you only notice incorrect behaviours and do not comment on correct ones.

Feedback can significantly affect motivation when the employee expects to receive it immediately. Feedback is best used when it is given daily, because daily doses of feedback will maintain the high performance level of your star performers. People want, crave and desire feedback. Feedback appeals to our human motivators of accomplishment and inner satisfaction.

In the absence of specific feedback, people invent their own performance standards. The only time people know what you are thinking is when you tell them. Silence leaves employees trying to figure out what is on your mind, and 99.9% of the time they are wrong.

Principle of Positive Consequences

If you spot a new behaviour that you would like the employee to continue, you must immediately call it to the attention of the employee and do so as soon as you notice it. You will see that employees are aware of their actions and that they will repeat the behaviour.

If you are not in the habit of providing daily feedback, it is necessary to boost your own confidence in giving feedback. When giving feedback is designed to improve performance, it is acceptable to use a model to guide you.

How to Keep Feedback Objective

Another reason people fear feedback is because they do not understand the difference between judging and describing. Much feedback is purely a judgement call on the giver's part. Your goal as coach and team leader is to identify those behaviours you would like employees to repeat and those that you want employees to alter or improve. This means that you must be able to clearly describe the specific behaviour to the employee and explain the positive or negative aspects of the behaviour without any biases. The following explains the difference between judging and describing.

Difference Between Judging and Describing

"I don't think you have the right attitude."	*This is a judgement statement of another person based on your beliefs or biases.*
"I saw you ignore Tom's request for help. Your job requires that you support Tom in his work."	*This is a describing statement explaining what you objectively observed without expressing an opinion.*

Types of Feedback

As mentioned earlier, managers frequently use feedback as criticism. This chart describes the four types of feedback, starting with silence. Even if you never give verbal feedback to employees, they still observe you to get some sense of what you think about their performance. Thus, even in silence you communicate to your employees. The other three are the more proactive forms of feedback, including the one that accountants fear the most: positive feedback. Members of the accounting profession, including those in public accounting, CFOs, and controllers, prefer silence, negative or neutral feedback. Figure 4-6 shows the comparison and effect of each type.

Figure 4-6: Four Types of Feedback

TYPE	ITS PURPOSE	ITS IMPACT ON THE EMPLOYEE
SILENCE *No feedback at all*	To maintain status quo	Diminishes confidence Unclarified expectations Creates surprise at reviews Creates paranoia and avoidance Fosters low accountability
CRITICISM *Negative feedback*	To stop undesirable performance or behaviour that does not meet a predefined standard	Generates excuses and blame Eliminates positive behaviour Decreases confidence Leads to escapism, avoidance Damages relationships
ADVICE *Neutral feedback*	To identify valued behaviours or results and specify how to use them or to shape behaviours	Improves confidence Improves relationship Increases performance Clarifies expectations
REINFORCEMENT *Positive feedback*	To identify behaviour or results already demonstrated and shape the continued use of them for increased performance	Increases confidence Improves performance Reinforces existing behaviours Taps into motivation Fosters full accountability

What Feedback Does

- Honours competence and reinforces behaviour
- Helps align expectations and priorities
- Fills gaps in people's knowledge
- Inform employees about problems to correct
- Alleviates fear of the unknown
- Fosters open communications
- Builds trust
- Rewards top performers
- Creates consequences for poor performers
- Establishes expectations and standards
- Creates a professional atmosphere
- Improves interdependence

How Leaders Use Feedback

- They just do it.
- They change unacceptable behaviour.
- They reinforce positive behaviour.
- They frequently and intimately give feedback.

- They focus it on the customer (internal or external).

- They find ways around the system if the culture does not value feedback.

- They first build a foundation with the person.

- They understand the difference between judging and describing.

- They give feedback on what is objective, that is, observable.

The Leader's Attitude Is Critical

The leader's attitude toward receiving feedback significantly affects their employee's attitude toward receiving feedback. We have all received criticism disguised as feedback. We knew that when the boss said, "Can I give you some feedback?" we would be chastised for something. If you do not believe in giving positive and neutral feedback, your employees will not either. If you believe in giving positive and neutral feedback and practise it daily, your employees will follow your example and give supportive feedback to one another.

Most leaders believe they do a good job of giving feedback. In reality, there is a huge discrepancy in getting and receiving feedback. The manager believes, "I am good at giving and asking for feedback and I listen to my employees." Employees say all too frequently, "I do not receive any feedback on how I am doing." and "No one listens to my feedback." The cause of this gap is the leader's ego, followed by the leader's hubris. Leaders need confidence in ourselves to make tough decisions and be accountable. But soon we believe our own press and think we never make mistakes or say the wrong thing. This is what creates a feedback gap. It is why you must jump-start the culture of feedback by seeking it for yourself from each member of your team.

How Feedback Uncovers Performance Problems Quickly

The following list provides some examples of hidden reasons why your employee may not be performing as expected. Notice how many would be uncovered by a daily dose of feedback given to the employee. Notice how many would linger if you waited for the annual performance evaluation to address the employee's performance. The employee

- does not know why he or she should do it.

- does not know how to do it.

- does not know what he or she is supposed to do.

- thinks your way will not work.

- thinks his or her way is better.

- thinks something else is more important.

- thinks no positive consequences exist for doing it.

- is rewarded for not doing it.

- is punished for doing what he or she is supposed to do.

- anticipates negative consequences for doing it.

- thinks no negative consequences exist for poor performance.

- has obstacles beyond his or her control.

- thinks personal limitations prevent him or her from performing.

- thinks no one can do it.

When and Where to Use Feedback

Feedback does not begin the moment an employee does something wrong.

It commences the day the employee starts working for you. The more you can provide feedback in the early stages of an employee's employment, the quicker you will shorten his or her learning curve and mould the employee into the star performer you believe he or she can be. In addition to orientation and training, the following are areas in which it is critical for you as a leader and coach to provide ongoing and supportive feedback:

- Orienting and training new employees
- Teaching a new set of job skills
- Explaining the standards of the department or unit
- Explaining cultural norms or political realities
- Correcting undesirable performance
- Changing goals or business conditions
- Adjusting to a new team
- Assisting employees in unfamiliar work experiences
- Helping new employees set priorities
- Following up on important training sessions
- Dealing with an employee with declining performance
- Reinforcing good performance
- Encouraging superior performance
- Conducting informal performance reviews
- Preparing employees to meet their future career goals
- Preparing employees for more challenging work assignments
- Building an employee's self-confidence
- Providing an emotional pick-me-up for an employee
- Building the team's cohesiveness in order to address conflict or power issues
- Leadership development programmes

Five Feedback Principles

1. The leader's primary concern is: Why do people resist attempts to adopt a different behaviour pattern?
2. The key to improving performance is to alter the person's behaviour.
3. People have an implicit cost-benefit analysis they use in any attempt to change their behaviour.
4. People refuse to change when they see that the change will cost them more than it will benefit them.
5. Employees create a psychological contract with their employer that implicitly and explicitly defines the terms of the exchange they expect. Employees fight when you change the terms of that psychological contract.

10½ Rules for Performance Improving Feedback

1. Observe the person in action.

2. Know what the proper behaviour is.

3. Identify the business reasons and use customer-based data.

4. Obtain the person's approval before proceeding.

5. Focus on the future.

6. Put feedback into a context the person can understand.

7. Remove anything that creates barriers and generates resistance.

8. Write descriptions of what the person is doing and what you want him or her to do. Be specific.

9. Discuss your feedback in private.

10. Allow plenty of time and keep it limited.

10½. Delay and you will never get improved performance.

In the End

In the absence of feedback, the employee creates his own standard of performance.

As a supervisor who wants to have a team of star performers, you must get in the habit of using feedback daily. Daily feedback results in quick improvements in performance when it is

- timely,
- caring, and
- honest.

The biggest benefit of using frequent feedback, especially the supportive and neutral type, is that you will be able to shape behaviours quickly. You will spot and alter the ones that harm productivity, quality or service and reinforce the behaviours that build interdependence as well as support productivity, quality or service.

Exercise: Are You a Champion?

Instructions

In each of the situations below answer "yes" only if this statement describes you in the workplace setting.

PART 1:	YES	NO
I spend a few minutes each day or each week with each employee providing them with specific feedback on how I see their performance.		
During performance evaluations there are no surprises because I have kept each employee apprised as to how well they have been performing their job responsibilities and their level of commitment to our team.		
PART 2:	**YES**	**NO**
When an employee offers to provide me a critique or feedback on something I have done that affects them, I say "yes" and carefully listen to what is on their mind without being defensive.		
If an employee provides me information through feedback I almost always take it to heart because there is a lesson in it for me.		
PART 3:	**YES**	**NO**
I do not wait for my scheduled performance evaluation to seek out information on how my performance is perceived by my managers and colleagues.		
I am open to any suggestions on how I can approve improve my own performance, especially from those who are at my level or above me.		

Answer Key

If a majority of your answers were "yes" in all three parts, then you believe in the power of feedback. Pay closer attention to the results that you immediately get after providing supportive feedback to someone. Notice also if you react or behave differently after receiving feedback. Teach others in your organisation about the importance of feedback.

If a majority of your answers were "no," you need to improve your commitment to providing timely feedback and obtaining it from others.

CFO Lesson

Without ongoing truthful feedback you create your own standards of performance and so do your employees.

BEST PRACTICE: SHAPE YOUR EMPLOYEES' BEHAVIOUR WITH RECOGNITION AND REWARDS

You must reinforce team behaviours to make them permanent.

Why Rewards and Recognition Foster Team Behaviours

It is important to reward individuals, and especially the team, when they deliver great service to those they serve. Behaviours that are rewarded are guaranteed to be repeated. You must always recognise every team member's contributions, especially when someone they serve acknowledges receiving great service or support.

Rewards Defined

Rewards that employees value most are those that clearly demonstrate recognition for their contributions. Too many managers and supervisors automatically think of monetary incentives or bonuses whenever the subject comes up. There are numerous ways of rewarding an employee for positive contributions besides giving them some cash. When given with sincerity and care, employees value simple things such as

- a thank-you card.
- recognition in the company newsletter.
- a pat on the back or a handshake.
- a handwritten note of thanks.
- acknowledging their contribution in a team meeting.
- certificate of appreciation.
- a small gift such as a gift certificate.
- being treated to lunch at the company's expense.
- special team events such as a pizza party or a bowling night.
- time off.
- a better parking space.

As leader of a team, avoid the habit of thinking that cash is the only reward or incentive available to you, which soon becomes the path of least resistance. Yes, employees do enjoy receiving an unexpected gift of money. However, the rewarding factor of cash disappears the moment the employee deposits the check or puts the cash in their wallet. A thank-you card from the supervisor stays visible a lot longer than a check for $25.00 because the employee will proudly tack the card up on the wall of his or her office space for others to see.

Recognition Defined

Recognition is a visible acknowledgment of performance. Every employee wants to be recognised for the positive ways that they add value. Because the work our management accounting teams do is typically invisible to everyone but us, it is more meaningful to a member of your team when you acknowledge something that many take for granted. Every day, members of your team are making their internal customers' jobs easier. Every time an employee offers a time savings idea or innovates an efficient process, you should give the person specific and sincere appreciation for his or her effort.

How Recognition Affects Performance and Value

A direct correlation exists between the recognition that an employee receives from their supervisor or from his or her peers and the level of his or her performance. The piece that links recognition to performance is the employee's self-esteem. When you increase the amount of recognition that you and others give to an employee, his or her self-esteem rises. When an employee's self-esteem rises, so does his or her productivity and effectiveness, which translates into positive performance.

Reinforcement Chain

Recognition is a basic human need. Therefore, to reinforce your employees behaviour so that they continue to provide positive performance, you must get in the habit of noticing them. Employees are a little like children— they want to be noticed. If a child is not being noticed, they may do something loud, obnoxious or against the rules in order to get attention. Similarly, your employees want to feel appreciated and liked by you. If you notice them often and provide the recognition they crave, you will automatically generate good behaviours and positive performance. If you do not notice them, they may act like children and create problems, forcing you to notice them.

By now, you might be thinking "I don't want to babysit my employees." Though you may be wary of the human element of leadership, you are not hand-holding your employee by recognising them. You are simply acknowledging the person as an asset to your team. This is what makes a leader effective in getting people to get from point A to point B.

Recognition Value Chain

A similar linking event occurs when you and others proactively provide recognition of the members within your team for their positive contributions.

You have begun to recognise a specific employee's performance. You observe that the employee is contributing more and living up to his customers' expectations. This improved performance continues to be noticed by team members and others. In turn, they acknowledge more of their co-workers' contributions and the level of positive recognition increases. Through this link to contributions, they become greater and more widespread. Therefore, the employee's positive contributions to others go up. The final link to the positive contributions is the value to the employee's team. In effect, just as the employee's self-esteem rises, so does the overall self-esteem of the team as a unit.

In summary, the way you build a valued team member is to begin to recognise on a daily basis the employee's positive contributions.

How Leaders Create Team Recognition

Recognition is a strategy for building a culture that rewards performance. The clever and effective controller or CFO desires to build a team culture that utilises recognition for others' contributions. Your overall recognition strategy is simple enough.

It starts with the employee. For example, when an employee experiences that you continually give him positive recognition for his contributions, he likes the way it feels. He also sees that he is treated better by his peers. He notices that other members of his team and the people he works with are doing small things that make his work easier and help him to be more effective. He begins to follow the example set by his supervisor and write thank-you notes, issue pats on the back, and provide little tangible gifts of thanks. He does this, not because it is expected of him, but because he likes the way he feels when acknowledged for something he did. He wants to pass this experience on to others. Most amazingly, he feels wonderful whenever he gives a sincere thanks to someone who helps him.

Very soon, everyone on the accounting team is giving each other positive strokes. It is now a team norm. Assuming that you work in a very functional culture, within a matter of months many others outside the accounting team are giving positive recognition to their employees and their peers and to those who serve them and vice versa. It is an amazing event to watch unfold.

Most importantly, all it took was one leader who believes in providing recognition as a form of rewarding the employee. The person who starts the ball rolling can be you.

How to Tap into the Power of Recognition

Recognition is driven by honest passion and caring. Managers and leaders who understand the power of recognition, its simplicity, its ease of implementation and its positive influence will be the most successful because they will apply recognition and actively encourage others in the organisation to do the same.

One of the important outcomes of recognition within an organisation is its ability to act as a facilitator and reinforcer of desirable behaviour.

Fourteen Behaviour/Reward Principles

1. What the organisation rewards communicates to employees what is really important.

2. Most organisations reward the wrong behaviours.

3. Behaviour that is rewarded is repeated.

4. How any one employee is rewarded and recognised affects the whole organisation.

5. Nearly all behaviours that negatively affect accountability can be traced to a reward that supports it.

6. The best reward, which provides the greatest incentive to maintain and improve performance, is the one that contributes to the fulfilment of the person's strongest motivator.

7. People will almost always take the path of least resistance, so the path must be changed to require someone to alter their behaviour.

8. Recognition is one of the most powerful job motivators available to the supervisor.

9. The effectiveness of recognition is in the attitude of the person giving it.

10. The less the culture values recognition, the harder it will be for people to embrace the new attitude.

11. If you work in a culture that prizes recognition, you will be more likely to give it to others, be aware of it and be gracious when you receive it.

12. If your culture does not favour recognition, you will limit the amount of it or decline to find ways to overcome the resistance to recognition.

13. Once a recognition programme is put into place, people still need to be regularly reminded of recognition.

14. Empowering individuals to recognise each other's contributions directly and immediately may be uncomfortable.

In the End

Behaviours that are rewarded are guaranteed to be repeated, so use this reality to build star performers on your team. Sincere recognition that you give to each employee for doing the small, important things that add value to others quickly will snowball into a team that provides one another with sincere recognition.

Exercise: Is It There?

Instructions

Be honest as you answer each question about your work setting.

		YES	NO
1.	When you walk through your work area, do you see lots of visible proof of recognition—objects like banners, pictures and bulletin boards recognising people's contributions?		
2.	Are employees able to play? Do you see items such as congratulatory parties, posters and mementos as visible proof that people take recognition playfully?		
3.	When asked, could employees provide a recent story about receiving, giving or personally observing recognition in action?		
4.	Is it evident within your team that the responsibility for giving out recognition belongs to everyone, not just the leader?		
5.	Are employees evaluated, in part, on the amount of recognition they give to others, especially those they work for and with?		
6.	On your team, are there tools and methods in place that allow employees to reward and honour each other?		

Answer Key

Each "Yes" answer reflects behaviours that support positive attitudes toward recognition.

Each "No" answer reflects a culture that does not value recognition.

CFO Lesson

Put your concentration on motivation, not compensation.

Exercise: Do You Believe in Feedback?

Instructions

Think about what you normally do at work when you witness both good and bad behaviours. Focus on your normal response to those situations.

With this in mind, complete the following analysis.

Part 1: When I spot a behaviour in any of my company's employees that should be improved or changed, but the employee is not someone I supervise, I use:

TYPE OF FEEDBACK	ALMOST ALWAYS	FREQUENTLY	OCCASIONALLY	NEVER
	APPROXIMATE % OF TIME USED			
Silence				
Criticism "That was not the way you were supposed to do that...."				
Advice "I noticed that you did... next time I suggest that you... ."				
Reinforcement "I noticed that you did ... and I really appreciate that...."				

Part 2: When I spot a behaviour in one of my employees that she should improve or change, I use:

TYPE OF FEEDBACK	ALMOST ALWAYS	FREQUENTLY	OCCASIONALLY	NEVER
	APPROXIMATE % OF TIME USED			
Silence				
Criticism "That was not the way you were supposed to do that...."				
Advice "I noticed that you did... next time I suggest that you...."				
Reinforcement "I noticed that you did ... and I really appreciate that...."				

Continued on p.104

Part 3: When I spot a behaviour in any employee that is admirable and worth repeating, I use:

TYPE OF FEEDBACK	ALMOST ALWAYS	FREQUENTLY	OCCASIONALLY	NEVER
	APPROXIMATE % OF TIME USED			
Silence				
Criticism "That was not the way you were supposed to do that...."				
Advice "I noticed that you did... next time I suggest that you...."				
Reinforcement "I noticed that you did ... and I really appreciate that...."				

Answer Key

While an exact assessment is difficult, you will quickly notice which of these four methods of feedback you use more and less frequently.

If, based on your answers, you discover that you mostly use silence or criticism, then you are undermining both your team's effectiveness and your own. You must change methods and become more supportive; you will find that you get a lot more positive results from your employees and those with whom you work.

CFO Lesson

You obtain better results by providing on a regular basis neutral and supportive feedback.

Part 4: Answer These Questions

What did you learn about yourself as a coach?

What areas of providing feedback do you need to improve to be more effective as a CFO?

5

STEP 5: IMPROVE YOUR CHANGE AGENT SKILLS THROUGH SELF-COACHING

You want to get ahead and show others that you can generate tangible results. To get there, you must assess where you are today and compare that to where you want to be. Once you have done that analysis, you will quickly grasp what you need to do between now and then so that you grow out of your job. In this step are four best practices that leaders universally use to obtain measurable results and live up to their self-determined expectations.

After reading this chapter, you should be able to

- explain to others the universal roles that the CFO plays in every organisation.
- use a gap analysis to quickly identify specific actionable steps to take.
- develop a formal action plan for strengthening accountability and ensuring execution.
- assess any gap you may have in your current skills as you move toward becoming a complete CFO.

YOUR NEED FOR SELF-COACHING

Everyone could use a little help.

These words of encouragement apply to the controller and CFO. Most of us know that we could be better at finishing what we start and achieving our goals. The coaching skills you applied to assist others you can now use on yourself. This chapter will cover some daily practices that will help you become even more effective as a catalyst for positive change.

Controller or CFO's True Role

From a bird's eye view, the head of the finance function in any organisation universally fulfils four interrelated roles:

1. Leader
2. Strategist

3. Culture shaper

4. Change agent

The first three roles were covered in previous chapters. As you assisted Brian in the exercise examples along the way, you worked on your fourth role.

Concurrent with those high level responsibilities, the CFO also carries out three tactical and very crucial duties in his or her organisation:

1. Team management

2. Corporate oversight

3. Fiscal management

As you fulfil these seven roles daily, you must feel confident relying on four resources that either make your job easier or more difficult. These assets are also universal to every CFO:

• People

• Systems

• Processes

• Rules

Figure 5-1 illustrates how these resources coalesce.

Figure 5-1: CFO's Universal Role Package

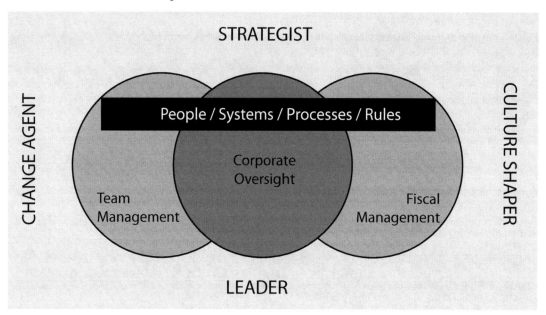

Similar Roles Yet Different Responsibilities

Despite these universal similarities, substantial differences exist in the responsibilities of the controller versus the CFO. At the end of this chapter is information that compares and contrasts the two roles in case one of your goals is to move from a controller to CFO or if you have the CFO or controller title but know that you could do more to serve your organisation's leadership needs.

BEST PRACTICE: SKILLS GAP ASSESSMENT

Exercise: Where Do You Score?

Instructions

Be completely honest and rate your ability in each of these skill areas. If you are unsure of the nature of the skill, read the explanation that follows.

CHANGE AGENT SKILL	I NEED TO WORK ON → I AM HIGHLY SKILLED								MY SCORE
	ENTER YOUR SCORE IN THE LAST COLUMN FOR EACH SKILL								
Active Listening	1	2	3	4	5	6	7	8	
Objective Observing	1	2	3	4	5	6	7	8	
Objectivity and Clarity	1	2	3	4	5	6	7	8	
Building Trust	1	2	3	4	5	6	7	8	
Testing Assumptions	1	2	3	4	5	6	7	8	
Partnering	1	2	3	4	5	6	7	8	
Problem Solving	1	2	3	4	5	6	7	8	
Integrative Thinking	1	2	3	4	5	6	7	8	
Selling Ideas	1	2	3	4	5	6	7	8	
Professionalism	1	2	3	4	5	6	7	8	
Taking a Firm Stance	1	2	3	4	5	6	7	8	
Total Score									

Answer Key

77–88—Congratulations! You are in great shape. Your next step is to coach and mentor others so they can develop these skills too.

66–76—You are employing your skills well. Your next steps are to seek out opportunities that will help you improve the skills on which scored yourself the lowest and obtain honest feedback from the people you serve. Use a gap analysis as your guide.

55–64—You are contributing and making differences in small areas. However, there are larger issues that you need to address. Your next step is to focus on the skills on which scored yourself the lowest and seek out opportunities to practise those skills until you have mastered them. Use a gap analysis as your guide.

44–54—You are only halfway to being an effective controller or CFO. The next steps you must take are to raise the bar for yourself and consider finding a mentor who will teach you the skills that you lack and challenge you to become more of who you can be. Use a gap analysis as your guide.

Below 44—You have a clear choice: (1) reevaluate your career choice, or (2) find ways to get out from behind your desk and become an agent of change each day, both inside your company and in volunteer situations.

Change Agent's Skills Explained

Active Listening

- When a person is actively listening, 100% of his or her being is involved.

- Hearing is a physiological reaction, while listening is a mental process.

Objective Observing

- Sitting back without an emotional attachment to what is in front of you and seeing it as a child would

- Observing or watching to see the entire picture and the parts that are not readily evident

Objectivity

- Staying above the problem or issue

- Not taking sides

Clarity

- Seeing the event or issue with fresh eyes

- Using all of your thinking abilities to see things holistically for insights and undiscovered truths

Building Trust

- Inspiring in others confidence in your ability and character

- Making others feel assured that you will not cause harm

Testing Assumptions

- Analysing your own or other peoples' assumptions surrounding an issue to identify and remove any biases

- Working to remove any paradigms that you use to filter out information that conflicts with your deeply rooted beliefs

Partnering

- Thinking and behaving collaboratively

- Keeping your employer's best interests in everything you do

Problem Solving

- Looking for solutions that not only stop the problem today but help to prevent it from occurring again tomorrow

- Using a wide variety of tools and insights to get to the core of the problem, while not getting bogged down in the side issues

Integrative Thinking

- Using facilitation tools to develop tailored and thoughtful recommendations for unique situations

- Learning quickly using a variety of methodologies

Selling Ideas

- Being able to convince or persuade someone with your arguments and logic

Professionalism

- Expecting that a person will act at a reliable level of integrity

- Expecting that a person will apply the full extent of his or her knowledge to an issue

Taking a Firm Stance

- Living up to your role as the conscience of your organisation

- Taking a firm stand against something that almost everyone else believes is a good choice

- Clearly stating your convictions and using that consistent stance to persuade others

BEST PRACTICE: GAP ANALYSIS

Gap Analysis Defined

A gap analysis is a visual examination of someone's current state compared to their desired state. A gap analysis starts with an honest assessment of where the person or organisation is today. It captures a clear vision of the future. The goal of your gap analysis is to demonstrate what is missing and required to reach this vision.

Steps for Preparing a Gap Analysis

In the description that follows, the client is the person who wishes to perform a gap analysis. The facilitator assists the client in doing so. Here, you serve as the facilitator.

1. Ask the client to describe the problem, issue or area on which he or she wants to make progress.

2. Ask the client to describe the reasons that he or she needs to solve this problem and why an action plan is needed for getting there.

3. If the client's dream is broad, ask him or her to focus on a particular aspect or element of the desired state. If the goal is too broad, the action plan will also be too broad.

4. Ask the client to define his or her deadline for achieving this desired state.

5. Ask the client to describe the current state of affairs as it relates to this end state or dream. Make sure that a balance exists of both assets or positives and the deficient areas. Keep the focus of today's status or reality on those things that contribute or detract from the desired end state. Work to keep your client honest and grounded.

6. Ask the client to describe what his or her destination will look like. Ask questions such as "What will you have? "What will it look like?" "How will it feel?" and "How will you know you have arrived?" Be sure to carry forward any acquired assets or positives into this future state.

7. Work with the client to fill in the middle section of the gap analysis, called the missing links. In as detailed a manner as possible, identify specific actions or steps that the client must take to go from today to tomorrow. If you completed your gap analysis correctly, these bridges will clearly pop out to both you and the client.

8. Use the information that you filled in as missing links or bridges to create a specific formalised action plan. Set a priority for each of the major action steps, often asking the question, "What must happen before you take this step?"

9. Review and update this gap analysis on a regular basis with the client. Use it to check progress and to see if there were other items in the missing links you or the client overlooked.

Exercise: Brian—Part 4

Instructions

Because you serve as Brian's coach, you will perform a gap analysis of Brian's skills as they are today. Brian provided you with this information and you will reciprocate by providing the missing links or bridges that Brian needs to cross the gaps.

Brian's area analysed: *Be promoted to CEO or COO*

BRIAN TODAY	THE MISSING LINKS	BRIAN IN 2 YEARS
Energetic		Energetic
Risk-taker		Risk-taker
Diplomatic		Diplomatic
Disciplined		Disciplined
Holds self accountable		Holds others accountable
Tenacious and goal-oriented		Tenacious and establishes others' goals
Works well with peers and employees		Works well with people at all levels
Executes until encounters an obstacle		Executes consistently
Somewhat visionary		Visionary
Loves selected challenges		Accepts all challenges well
Adequate communicator		Leader communication style
Avoids direct confrontation		Direct and assertive
Views problems only in financial terms		Views problems from a strategic holistic level
Great grasp of managing a team		Inspiring and empowering leader
Great grasp of finance, budgets and business		Great grasp of running a business

About Your Friend Brian

Brian optimistically believes that the ultimate solution to saving R & K is to be placed in charge or have more influence over the R & K Enterprise. Brian would then be more successful in removing almost all the challenges. Brian thinks the biggest payoff for the families in allowing Brian to take on such a role would be that they would have something valuable to sell or pass on to their children.

Assume that Ruwan, Kimberley and the associated family members have agreed with Brian's assessment and are willing to make the changes in leadership that Brian envisions. You can assume that Ruwan and Kimberley will support what Brian suggests so that in the next 24 months Brian will be given the opportunity to take over leadership of the enterprise.

Your Task

Now that you have prepared Brian's agenda for the next year, it is time to assist Brian in defining where improvements are needed.

As you fill in the middle section of Brian's gap analysis, place yourself in this situation and ask yourself this question:

What would you do to gain the experience and confidence that is required to fulfil the dream state on the right column of Brian's gap analysis?

In the End

The gap analysis is a fantastic best practice that every CFO should have in his or her toolkit. By getting into the habit of using it as you set goals and take on projects, you will quickly be able to grasp the items that you need to move from where you are today to where you want to be tomorrow. It is a very powerful and insightful tool which will help you execute your goals and achieve your vision.

Exercise: Apply Your Learning

Create a gap analysis of your situation as it exists today. Be honest. Start with the "You Today" column.

Problem, issue or skill area analysed: _____

_____

When is tomorrow? _____ from today.

YOU TODAY	THE MISSING LINKS	YOU TOMORROW

BEST PRACTICE: FORMALISED ACTION PLAN

The biggest payoff from using formalised action plans is the ability to communicate accountability to people.

Obtain Tangible Results With an Action Plan

Action Plan Defined

A tool of great value for consistent execution is the formalised action plan (FAP) (figure 5-2). An action plan is a visual definition or map of what it will take to make significant progress on a specific objective. Use this tool to model and convert your tactics into specific action steps to ensure you achieve all of your goals.

Figure 5-2: A Formalised Action Plan or Initiative

Overall Strategic Goal: Dispose of obsolete and dropped inventory products profitably.

Measurable Strategic Plan Tactic: Reduce inventory by 20% and improve the turnover from four turns to six turns.

Connection to our Risk Management Programme

In the company's risk management programme, we have addressed the concern that as a new company we have not established sufficient protocols and controls to deal with obsolete inventories. We acknowledged in the risk management programme that we currently are in a negative cash flow position and will be for the next 18 months. Therefore, our inherent risk is that we may focus too much attention on managing cash, accounts receivable and accounts payable and not enough attention on the balance sheet items unrelated to immediate cash flows.

Major Action Steps

1. Implement a plan to dispose of all aged inventory.
2. Implement a plan to dispose of all dropped products.
3. Establish controls to ensure the products are sold for their highest value.
4. Establish a way to provide an incentive for a sales employee to sell old products without hurting the sales of current products.

Anticipated Obstacles and Challenges

1. Assigning the responsibilities to sell and ship the products to an already overworked staff.
2. Finding an inexpensive way to move inventory from the Ohio warehouse to the buyer.
3. Protecting the company's reputation, while disposing of obsolete products.
4. Convincing our suppliers to take back some products and issue credits.
5. Paying adequate incentive compensation to employees who sell the inventory, as there will be no profit margin to the company.
6. Determining the negative financial impact of the disposal and communicating this to the board and the bank.
7. Keeping the momentum needed to fully dispose of all obsolete products while keeping losses low.

Detailed Activities or Tasks

1. Select the products for disposal.

2. Ask the purchasing manager to provide an analysis of the returnability of the dropped products.

3. Contact any companies who buy our products, or products like ours, in bulk.

4. Hire a telemarketing person to handle the sale of smaller quantities.

5. Establish commission or incentive plans for product sales.

6. Determine the approval levels for authorising sale prices.

7. Prepare weekly updates on the status of sales and negotiations.

Change Team

Change Agents:

Sponsor:

Advocate:

The contents of FAP include the following items:

- Overall strategic objective
- Deliverables
- Due dates
- Major steps
- Detailed steps
- Individual responsibilities
- Anticipated obstacles and challenges
- Performance metrics
- Resources required (financial and nonfinancial)

Every FAP should define each level of change responsibility at the outset.

FAP participants include the following:

- *Sponsor*—Person who has ultimate accountability for the change, typically pays for the project through the budget
- *Advocate*—Person who drives, wants or demands the change
- *Customers*—Person(s) who benefit from the change
- *Agents of Change*—Persons who carry the responsibility for facilitating the change through to the end
- *Accountability Partner*—Person—executive or senior leader—who will help to hold the change agent's feet to the fire; not quite a mentor, the change agent regularly reports back to this person about the progress made toward the plan's ultimate objective

FAPs are used for

- highlighting overall objectives.
- connecting tasks to the ultimate objective.
- spelling out each participant's role in the change.
- setting forth expected or desired results.
- keeping track of actual results.
- holding employees to task.
- clarifying expectations.
- identifying risks and obstacles in advance.

Result

Using this FAP, the team was able to remove the problem and establish a new sustainable protocol for dealing with obsolescence in less than five months.

BEST PRACTICE: ACTION PLAN REPORTING AND ACCOUNTABILITY

The Action Plan Reporting and Accountability tool (figure 5-3) complements the FAP because it raises the plan's visibility and measures its progress. On a regular basis, require the FAP's sponsor or champion to report on the plan's status. Requiring that the change team measures the plan's financial impact ensures that the focus is on results together with the cost of getting those results—a balanced approach to instilling ethical conduct.

Figure 5-3: Action Plan Summary

EMPLOYEES INVOLVED	ACTION PLAN'S STRATEGIC GOAL	EXPECTED FINANCIAL RESULTS		ACTUAL RESULTS	
		INCREASED SALES $$	(DECREASED) EXPENSES $$	FINANCIAL AS OF APRIL 30, 2012	NONFINANCIAL
Sponsor— Advocate— Customers— Agents—	Dispose of obsolete and dropped inventory products profitably	$5,000	$7,580		
Sponsor— Advocate— Customers— Agents—					

EMPLOYEES INVOLVED	ACTION PLAN'S STRATEGIC GOAL	EXPECTED FINANCIAL RESULTS		ACTUAL RESULTS	
		INCREASED SALES $$	(DECREASED) EXPENSES $$	FINANCIAL	NONFINANCIAL
				AS OF APRIL 30, 2012	
Sponsor— Advocate— Customers— Agents—					
Sponsor— Advocate— Customers— Agents—					

Definitions:
 Sponsor—the person who has the ability to pay for the change.
 Advocate—the person who wants or demands the change.
 Customers—the recipients who benefit from the change.
 Agents—the persons responsible for facility the change.

In the End

A FAP can powerfully help the controller meet obligations and hold others accountable to their commitments. Build the habit of using this best practice for all your projects and major tasks which take time and involve others. Once you get comfortable using the FAP, teach it to others so they can benefit from it as well.

CFO Versus the Controller—How the Roles Vary

The CFO and the controller usually are the personnel most intimately involved in meeting an organisation's fiscal or financial goals and objectives. The responsibilities of the CFO are broader and extend far beyond just the finance department.

Typically more externally oriented, a CFO is concerned with organisation-wide and marketplace issues. As an executive with a deep understanding of finance and broad-based business knowledge who serves on the leadership team, the CFO is responsible for bringing the financial point of view to the forefront when his or her organisation makes its most crucial decisions. The board and owners—for instance, shareholders or members—look to their CFO to establish, maintain and monitor the vital governance programme.

The controller generally is more narrowly focused on the issues and obligations of the finance department, administration areas and, most critically, the internal control structure. Although the controller's responsibilities may be narrower than a CFO's, a good controller must be prepared to back up his or her CFO. Wise controllers will develop a deep understanding of how their organisation works and offer the necessary skills to support their CFO's responsibilities.

Both financial professionals must be viewed as business partners and, therefore, take a proactive role by participating in both management and operational decision making.

As the chart that follows illustrates, the CFO and controller positions can be seen as quite different in their scope and orientation. It is unwise to assume that someone with controller experience can automatically move into the role of the CFO or that someone who has been a CFO is also excellent at a controller's responsibilities. Some organisations prefer a CFO who is not a CPA, ACMA or FCMA to ensure that he or she lacks a "bean counter" mentality.

Responsibility Comparison

Figure 5-4 portrays the overall responsibilities of these two important roles. Notice that the CFO must take ownership of global and firm-wide issues while the controller must take ownership of the accounting team and its impact on finances and service.

Figure 5-4: Scope Responsibility Comparison

SCOPE OF RESPONSIBILITY	CFO	CONTROLLER*
Have concern for the marketplace	Very important	Important
Have a global organisational awareness	Very important	Important
Have a board orientation	Very important	Important
Be the management team builder	Very important	Important
Be the fiscal policy setter	Very important	Important
Implement the governance programme	Very important	Important
Be the strategist	Very important	Important
Be the change agent	Very important	Very important
Serve as communication nexus	Very important	Very important
Be the firm's conscience	Very important	Very important
Instil an attitude of service in finance	Very important	Very important
Establish the culture	Very important	Important
Be the financial policy setter	Important	Important
Build the finance team	Important	Very important
Be the efficiency expert	Less important	Very important
Be the expert in finance and accounting standards	Less important	Very important
Know each team member's effectiveness	Less important	Very important
Be the work organiser	Less important	Very important

*This comparison assumes that the controller reports to a CFO. If the leader of the finance function, especially in a small organisation, serves as both controller and CFO, then many of the responsibilities designated for a CFO must be assumed by the controller.

Functional Role Comparison

The roles of the CFO and controller must complement each other, with each person bringing his or her unique skill set to the table so that together they fulfil an essential organisational function, what is referred to in the encompassing term "management accounting." Figure 5-5 shows a sample functional role comparison.

Figure 5-5: Functional Role Comparison

MAJOR FUNCTIONAL AREA	CFO'S ROLE	CONTROLLER'S ROLE*
Financial Reporting (external feedback)	Identifies external reporting needs; presents and explains financial reports.	Prepares external financial reports.
Management Reporting (internal feedback)	Develops framework on ways and means for reporting; provides a common focus on key performance indicators that measure the firm's strategy.	Develops appropriate reporting structure; prepares reports and weds financial and nonfinancial data; provides a monthly State of the Union.
Treasury Management	Develops overall treasury strategy in line with operational and capital plans; maintains ongoing and open relationships with investors and bankers.	Monitors and supervises asset balances, investments, borrowings and fund transfers.
Risk Management	Assesses exposure and calculates firm's risk tolerance; determines insurance coverage requirements.	Administers insurance portfolio; provides risk assessment tools to employees.
Budgeting	Establishes broad budget parameters based on the strategic plan; presents budget to board and executive council for review and approval.	Facilitates the budget process; aids in the development of detailed budgets based upon operating plan; monitors overall budget.
Strategic Planning	Sponsors or manages the annual planning retreat; represents finance's interests in plans; presents overall financial picture to board and executive council.	Prepares analyses and information to be used by retreat participants.
Performance Analysis	Identifies operational and financial areas to be measured; establishes success factors; establishes firm-wide scorecard; reviews actual performance against targets with board and executive council.	Designs, prepares and distributes operational, financial, statistical and other reports that measure actual performance against targets.

*This comparison assumes that the controller reports to a CFO. If the leader of the finance function, especially in a small organisation, serves as both controller and CFO, then many of the roles designated for a CFO may fall to the controller.

The CFO's functional role is to help define the big picture and develop or assist in developing global strategies that carry out the organisation's mission. The controller then uses his or her resources and technical knowledge to execute those strategies with specific tactics. Through the controller's reporting responsibility, the executive team obtains timely feedback regarding its strategy's viability and employees' efforts to carry out designated tactics.

While both positions serve as a vital communication nexus, the CFO essentially fulfils the role as the main interface between the finance function and the board or executive team and between the finance function and the shareholders. On the other hand, a controller is the main interface between the finance function and all internal departments and between the finance function and most external stakeholders (for instance, IRS, vendors and so forth).

Valuing and Choosing the Appropriate Role

As a CFO, you can either choose the role that brings out the best in you or let the employer define a role for you. The following chart demonstrates that there are multiple levels within each role that the CFO and controller can play.

Take time to study figure 5-6 and evaluate which role matches what you want to accomplish as a management accounting leader. Pay attention to the ways in which the values in the two roles vary.

Figure 5-6: Role Valuation Comparison

ROLE	DESCRIPTION
Owner Adviser	Works closely with the organisation's owner(s) and becomes their personal counsellor. Seeks external financing for growth, recapitalisation or planned IPO.
Strategist	Assists in establishing overall strategy the organisation must take to be successful. This role is required in small companies that have absentee leadership or an owner who lacks ability to think and act strategically.
Compliance Officer	Serves as the rule enforcer in the organisation where no one else serves that purpose.
Chief Operating Officer Controller	Assists in nontraditional matters and serves as a key member of leadership team. Usually found in small organisations.
Financial or Acting CFO Controller	Operates as CFO in addition to administrating typical accounting functions.
Operational Controller	Helps manage the organisation in addition to administrating accounting functions. This role is required in small organisations with absentee leadership or owners with limited leadership roles.
Accounting Controller	Does bookkeeping and basic accounting work. Often found in large organisations.

6

STEP 6: IMPROVE YOUR SKILLS AS A LEADER IN THE MIDDLE

As the conscience of your organisation, you must be able to find lasting solutions. The downfall of many controllers, CFOs and finance directors is that they are so busy fighting fires that they are unable to devote time to preventing those fires. This step illuminates the real hurdle and its sources that you must face and overcome. It also provides valuable tools that will enable you to use your objective reasoning and business acumen to be a creator of solutions.

After reading this chapter, you should be able to

- define why being a leader in the middle is not a career limiter.
- become a more effective problem solver.
- increase your comfort level in using probing questions.
- restate an apparent problem in different ways to find an optimal solution.

This chapter is designed to help you grow out of your job. You accomplish this step by developing and enhancing your skills through practice and application of new tools. Make sure that one of the things you commit to from this day forward is to see yourself as a lifelong learner. This step includes ways to survive as a leader in the middle and three best practices for optimal solutions.

Exercise: Case Study—You?

You have been very successful in coaching Brian. But while Brian's problems are theoretical, yours are not. As we cover this sixth step, think about how you can use this exercise to become a solution creator for yourself.

Instructions

Part 1: List the top six issues that are preventing you from being more effective. Lack of time is not a valid answer; it is an excuse or a crutch.

1. _____

2. _____

3. _____

4. _____

Continued on p.120

Part 2: Examine these six items objectively.

Now, briefly describe your pain.

I see now that my pain is...

(Examples: "Putting my needs last." "Procrastination." "Not asking my boss for what I need to be successful." "Not addressing employees who are not contributing.")

Part 3: How would you define the true issue that is stopping you?

The real issue, hidden behind the smokescreen of ongoing fires and lack of time, is...

YOUR PERSONAL STRENGTH: SURVIVING AS A MANAGER IN THE MIDDLE

Playing at or being the leader is much more fun than learning or practising at how to be one.

Your Biggest Hurdle to Becoming a Great Leader

For the majority of management accountants who felt the urge to walk through the leadership door or have found themselves in a situation in which they had to be a leader, there is a huge hurdle to overcome. This hurdle is the most difficult part of management accounting leadership, which is moving from knowing what you need to do to really doing it.

Your organisation expects you to perform high-level work and lead a team. However, it's likely that you are not given the support and time needed to carry out either of these major functions well. In addition, you are often very knowledgeable about what is best for your organisation, yet your colleagues and leadership may not ask you or take your advice seriously.

The good news is that every great controller and CFO has overcome this hurdle, and so can you. Following are the causes of the manager in the middle syndrome and how you can overcome this major hurdle.

Sources of Your Most Difficult Hurdle

This hurdle has four sources, which together or individually most often prevent you from being the leader you know yourself to be and the team needs you to be. Each arises from middle leader issues you face daily.

Source 1: Your Employees

A misplaced or disheartened employee says, "I hate it here but am stuck until I can afford to retire." A situation like this will produce problematic results if you do not address it while building a productive and reliable team. You will have people on your team whose heart is not in their work and are terrified to leave. As leader, you must address this problem and ensure that all employees contribute their best work. The true CFO knows that by setting high expectations and holding every employee to them, you set the tone that everyone, including you, must perform each day at 100%. Then you compassionately and directly work on each person's attitude and remind them to stay positive.

Remember to include the following leadership rule in your efforts.

Natural Rule of Leadership

A leader must never allow the negative attitude of one individual or a small group to infect the positive attitude of the majority. If the majority has the negative attitude, you must change how you quickly lead or let someone else lead. Your real issue could stem from one or more of the following:

- *Upset or disgruntled employee*—Accountants may shy away from confrontation, which indicates you are hesitant to lead. A CFO addresses a conflict immediately. You must always quickly deal with an upset or unpleasant employee with the goal of turning that person back into a contributing member of your team.

- *Underperforming long-term employee*—You may have inherited a performance problem created or ignored by another supervisor. Not facing up to and fixing this situation is like trying to safely drive a car with one flat tire: impossible. A good CFO knows that in a team setting, one bad apple eventually will spoil the whole bunch.

- *Inadequate Training*—Even if you do not think you have the funds or time to train your team members, you damage your credibility as a leader when you have poorly trained or under-trained employees. You cannot accomplish your work alone, and you must surround yourself with people who know more than you do. The CFO always finds ways to turn work activities into learning opportunities.

Source 2: Your Work

The great CFO and everyone else all face similar work, which can be demanding and is time-sensitive. However, you should never let the urgent crowd out the important.

Deadline pressures—The great number of deadlines we face makes them seem to be the most urgent matters your team must work on today. However, more important duties are in your leadership in-basket, such as building a high quality and loyal team. Great CFOs turn deadlines into something meaningful, which, in turn, helps their employees enjoy the work.

Repetitiveness and boredom—Repetition is supposed to build perfection. Yet poor leaders allow the necessity of doing the same work over and over produce boredom, inappropriate short-cuts, inattention and passivity. The leader in management accounting uses the nature and volume of the work as a catalyst for measurable improvement and a commitment to quality.

Massive quantity and never-ending flow—Similar to the problems created by repetitiveness, the unfortunate fact that most of us have more work than people can harm our credibility. A CFO shows poor leadership by not using this situation as a catalyst for the team to focus on cross-training, streamlining and simplifying. A CFO challenges his or her team to find ways to become lean so it has more time to work on activities that personally are meaningful and rewarding.

Source 3: Your Firm's Culture

The culture is an area in which too many management accountants let the manager-in-the-middle syndrome defeat them.

The accomplished CFO restructures any part of the firm's culture that undermines the effectiveness of his or her team. Even if you feel you cannot change your employer's overall culture, you already (*a*) affect this culture and (*b*) set the tone for your department's culture. As someone who wants to be an effective leader, you must take charge of changing cultural norms so your team feels like winners, not losers.

- *Lack of external support*—Using your leadership talents as negotiator, change agent and role model, you must build support for your team's efforts one fan at a time. Management accounting is sometimes looked down upon by people who do not know any better. Your duty as leader is to teach others that the management accounting team is vital to the organisation's overall success.

- *Demanding employer*—Many of us work for entrepreneurs who push themselves hard and expect everyone else to work impossible hours and weekends. Yet you and your team members want to have time for family and activities outside of work. Here, an excellent CFO can show assertiveness and care. As team leader, it is up to you to find the appropriate balance between commitment to the firm and to the individual. Once you find it, you must protect it and, when needed, stand up for your employees' rights and needs.

Source 4: You

We can and do undermine our desire to be great. Following are areas in which the true leaders have learned to stop getting in their own way.

- *No Sounding Board*—To be a great leader, you must seek out honest feedback regarding your effectiveness. The following are common excuses management accountants give when asked to consider using a coach or mentor:

  ◦ "I don't have time."

  ◦ "I know how I am doing."

  ◦ "I can't trust anyone to tell me the truth."

  ◦ "He (she) will only tell me the bad things I am doing."

  ◦ "I don't trust anyone that much."

  ◦ "I work alone most of the time."

  All of these are false excuses that tell me the individual is afraid.

  The great CFO knows that having a sounding board goes beyond using one to obtain honest feedback on your leadership abilities. The management accounting leader in a typical organisation may feel isolated for a variety of reasons. You will always need someone to bounce ideas off and provide suggestions, critiques and insights. Unless you work in an organisation where you have multiple peers who perform the same work that you do, you will not have access to peer support. It is up to you to seek out and recruit a mentor or coach.

- *Too many projects*—Because of your multiple responsibilities, you may burn yourself out. All CFOs know that they need to regularly relax to refresh and replenish. It is acceptable to be a Type A leader if your busyness produces excellent results while still building a great team. It is not wise to be busy if you never produce anything great.

- *Misspent or wasted energy*—Just as being overly busy can make you an ineffective leader, so can applying your precious energy in the wrong areas. The CFO treats his or her energy like a cash investment. Each investment of energy must be wise and produce a measurable or meaningful payoff. If the benefit does not exceed the cost, rethink what you are working on or turn to your sounding board for clarity.

BEST PRACTICE: SOLUTION CREATOR

How to Be an Effective Problem Solver

Whenever acting as a solution creator, keep in mind the following points:

- The CFO's initial goal is to uncover the person's pain.
- The CFO's ongoing objective is to build a strong relationship of trust.
- The CFO treats each person as a client in order to maintain a professional approach to problem solving.
- The CFO's professional demeanor helps him or her to find realistic and innovative solutions for the client.
- The CFO's professional demeanor helps build a relationship of trust with those who rely on the CFO's acumen and insight.
- The CFO strives to be an equal partner with the other person because a partnership means that each party is invested in the relationship.
- The person you help rarely knows what the source of their pain is because he or she is too close to the action to see things objectively. This is when the CFO becomes invaluable.

The following are your most valuable tools for uncovering your employer's pain:

- Gap analysis
- Probing questions
- Problem restatement

Their Pain Is Real and Tangible, Yet Hidden

The term "pain," in this context, means that your organisation's executives, managers and employees have unresolved problems. As the controller or CFO, you are the logical choice and most qualified person to help rid them of their pain. You understand how the business operates, you understand how the finances work, and you understand the key players and what makes them tick. One of the most rewarding aspects of the CFO position is to be regarded as the resource that employees think of first when they need a solution.

This does not mean that your coworkers and colleagues will get answers from you.

What you will do best is employ your tools to help them find their own solutions. The last thing you want is to place yourself in a position in which you cannot get your own work done because you are always solving everyone else's problems. An effective way to avoid this career-limiting situation is to see yourself as a consultant to others in the organisation. Good consultants best serve their client when they enable the client to arrive at his or her own solution to a problem and instils accountability in the client. In order to do so effectively, you must ensure that others trust you.

BEST PRACTICE: PROBING QUESTIONS

How to Get to the Real Problem

The CFO uses probing questions to uncover the sources of the pain. You poke and prod until the person says "ouch." The solution you seek starts there.

The reason you seek the pain point is because the people who need a solution knows a problem exists but is unable to resolve it on their own. They have a goal or destination that they want to reach. Not being able to get there leaves them very frustrated, so they naturally are defensive. If you use direct questioning, they will likely become defensive, leaving them unable to locate the real causes for their pain.

Power in Probing Questions

Probing questions (PQs) are critical to the CFO because they do the following:

- Encourage people to think and unlock untapped potential

- Allow people to discover their own answers, thus transferring ownership

- Mine the real experts—the employees—for their gold

- Help people realise how the work they do contributes to the whole

- Help people feel fulfilled, satisfied and valued

- Build positive attitudes and self-esteem

- Remove blocks and open people up to unexplored possibilities while inviting discovery, creativity and innovation

- Help people envision what it will take to do what they have not attempted before

- Guide people toward where they want to go, while recognising the value in where they are and have been

- Involve people in the decision making process, generating commitment to solutions

- Generate alignment with a shared vision or desired outcome

- Encourage people to identify, clarify and express their wants and needs

- Encourage people to take risks

- Recondition people from knowing what to think to knowing how to think

- Nurture a deeper relationship and engender trust

- Dissolve resistance to change

- Create a high-energy, high-trust environment

Fundamentals of PQs

- PQs are open-ended.

- PQs ask "What" or "How" instead of "Why" or "Who."

- PQs are you-oriented.

- PQs show that the questioner is open and willing to hear the answer—whatever it may be.

- PQs are framed to fit the situation and clarify what is required.

- PQs help people learn through the process of answering.

- PQs give a person credit for their answer, whether they know something or not.

- PQ's can be shaped to fit the situation.

- PQ's aid the learning process.

- PQ's start out broad and general, then can be made more specific with each answer you receive.

Exercise: Examples of Structured Probing Questions

Assume that you are trying to understand why an employee, John, has missed a deadline or does not appear to you to take an action plan seriously. You would naturally want to hold this person accountable.

If you begin the conversation with confrontation, the employee will become defensive and may not be honest about this situation.

Try using the following questions to uncover and understand all the facts so you can enable the employee to become part of the solution.

Ask your employee:

What was the original deadline?

What were you able to accomplish?

How well do you think that you met the desired outcome?

What interfered with your meeting this outcome?

Based on what you did accomplish, what would you do the next time this occurs?

You may be thinking "Why not ask him if he completed it?" or "Why not ask him what is left to be done?" or "Why not ask him why he didn't finish the project as requested?"

If you go to the heart of the matter before you uncover any facts, you risk not getting a straight answer. If the employee is feeling the least bit of shame about not meeting the deadline, he most likely will lie to you or minimise what is left undone. Also, you may not be aware of other circumstances. For instance, your boss, unbeknownst to you, gave him a rush project and he failed to inform you, assuming your boss would do so.

In other words, boldly and blindly going into your accusations through direct and pointed questions about his alleged or assumed lack of professionalism could damage the trust you have built with him.

Why Management Accountants Do Not Use Objective Questioning

For whatever reason, built into the personality structure of the person drawn to management accounting is often the desire to get to the bottom line quickly. So the questions to ask others in order to assist them with their problems are often pointed and filled with assumptions about the situation. While this approach may seem economical and timesaving, it rarely is effective.

The following change agent skills heavily rely on the usage of probing questions:

- Active listening

- Objective observing

- Testing your assumptions

- Integrative thinking
- Selling your ideas

Use Probing Questions as a Wedge

Start by asking questions that are general in nature and then move to more specific ones. These latter questions will take you to the heart of the matter. The tone of your questions must show that you are open to listening and desire to find the cause of the issue without specifically blaming the person you are questioning. Follow the format in figure 6-1.

Figure 6-1: Format for Probing Questions

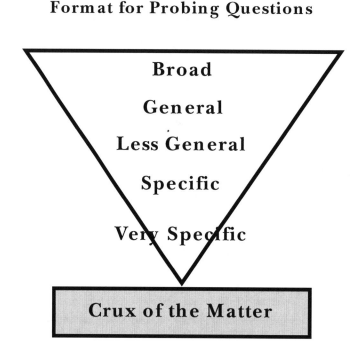

People naturally or habitually seek expediency rather than objectivity, as shown in the following exercise.

Exercise: What Questions Do You Prefer?

Instructions

Assume the same situation applies as in the previous example: you are talking to an employee who you suspect might be underperforming. Consider these two sets of questions and how you would react if your supervisor posed them to you.

Set One

Why are you behind schedule?

What is your problem?

Why didn't you complete your action plan?

Who on your team is not doing their fair share of work?

Why did you make that mistake?

Set Two

How do you feel about your current goals?

What have you recently accomplished of which you are very proud?

What are your specific objectives for this project?

What key things do you need to achieve your objectives?

What have you learned about the work you completed so far?

CFO Lesson

Questions are designed to commence dialogue and foster mutual trust. However, your question's phrasing will either open or close honesty in the dialogue. Badly phrased questions harm trust and your credibility. Yet we almost always use the first set of questions and then wonder why people do not trust us enough to be completely open and honest.

BEST PRACTICE: PROBLEM RESTATEMENT

Your assumptions drive everything that follows.

How management accountants analyse a problem absolutely determines whether they find a solution and the quality of that solution. Often in hindsight they find the initial definition of the problem was off the mark. The reasons they didn't permanently solve the problem—if they even tried to solve it at all—are the following:

- Every problem can be viewed from conflicting perspectives.
- Biases are the unseen killer of the objective truth.
- Biases determine our perspective, which drives our analysis, which generates our conclusions and recommendations.

Therefore, the CFO using objective thinking strives to identify any biases he or she and others have from the outset.

Exercise: Example of Biased Reasoning

This frustrated couple is having a conversation about their son. Notice how they deal with their plight.

Father:	"He does not apply himself."
Mother:	"I know. He really isn't interested. His mind wanders."
Father:	"I'm tired of nagging him all the time."
Mother:	"Me too. It does not seem to have any effect."
Father:	"Maybe he needs tutoring in how to study."

Continued on p.128

Mother:	"It couldn't hurt. He has terrible study habits."
Father:	"I'll call the school tomorrow and arrange something."
Mother:	"Good. I'm sure it will help him."

Answer These Questions:

How did the parents define the problem?

Are lack of interest and mind wandering the problem?

What are other ways to see this issue? What other causes of the problem could there be?

Did the parents own up to the problem or distance themselves from it? Are they accountable?

Ways Get to the Real Cause of an Issue or Problem

The real issues, which are the root cause of someone's lingering problem, are often hidden. They may be hidden behind a veil of smoke because of

- excessive ego,

- fear of failure,

- fear of incompetence,

- true incompetence, or

- game playing for power.

Understanding the cause of smoke screens aids the CFO in seeing behind them and discovering the source of the fire.

No. 1 Big Mistake of the CFO

Not defining the problem accurately

CFOs fall into this trap when they are so focused on the passing of time and deadlines that they aim for expediency over everything else. As a CFO you cannot afford to make this mistake often.

Information for defining the real problem or issue comes from the following sources:

- Your personal knowledge

- Your expertise

- Discussions with the person who needs or demands the solution

- Discussions with the people who are affected by the problem and will be affected by the solution

- Gap analysis or similar assessment

- Investigation or audit of the systems, processes, or documents involved

- Your intuition

You err if you heavily rely on only one of these sources of information. You may be comfortable in using what has worked for you in the past and hesitate to rely on other assets or tools. Review this list again and determine which of these talents or assets you most heavily rely on to the exclusion of the others.

No. 2 Big Mistake of the CFO

Not using others to sound out your reasoning or logic

You may encounter this trap when you do not test your reasoning with others who are not involved in the problem. You make this mistake for three reasons.

1. You are in a hurry.
2. You have not built or used a network of peers.
3. You do not think that you need to.

No matter how intelligent or experienced, all CFOs need a way to sound out their reasoning or logic. Doing so is not an admission that you are incompetent, something that most professionals secretly fear. Rather, it is an enlightened practice.

When you turn to someone you trust and know can remain objective, you are simply asking them to look for flaws, biases or assumptions in your thought process. As human beings we all have biases. These assumptions about how life works interfere with your ability to be objective and work to find the optimal solution to a problem.

Never be afraid to ask others to be your sounding board and to help you clarify your thinking so that you remain objective. This is an important trait of the successful CFO.

How to Use Problem Restatement

Problem restatement is defined as restating the problem in as many ways as possible. As you restate the problem several times, you shift your mental gears into a divergent thinking mode. To restate a problem successfully, you take time to generate written statements of the problem without evaluating or solving it.

Exercise: Problem Restatement Case Study

The Painful Problem—The parking lot outside our office building is packed with employees' cars. Every space is taken and a number of employees have to park elsewhere. This situation generates a lot of complaints.

Getting to a Solution—Having decided to eliminate this problem, our executive team convenes a task force to tackle it. The task force is given the responsibility of devising alternative ways of redesigning the parking lot to hold more cars.

The task force comes up with six different alternatives to increase the lot's capacity.

It is easy to use the problem restatement tool when you get into the habit of following these six steps.

The Process for Restating the Problem

1. Use "How to…" to start defining the issue as an answer to the question.

2. Paraphrase the problem without shifting the primary focus.

   - "How to increase the number of parking spots near the office."
   - "How to increase the number of cars that can park in the lot without increasing the number of parking spaces."

3. Make a 180-degree shift in the problem's focus by viewing it from the opposite angle.

   - "How to reduce the number of cars that park in the lot."
   - "How to transport people to work without using automobiles."

4. Simplify the wording.

   - "How to increase the lot's current capacity."

5. Make each statement positive and remove any negative and inflammatory words.

   - "How to not decrease the capacity while not impacting availability."

   Revise the statement from the previous step.

   - "How to equalise the number of cars with the space available."

6. Use active statements.

   - "How to ensure each employee has a place to park."

Exercise: Restate This.

List some possible solutions generated by the specific problem definitions.

"How to increase the number of cars that park in the lot without increasing the number of parking spaces."

"How to reduce the number of cars that park in the lot."

"How to transport people to work without using automobiles."

"How to equalise the number of cars with the spaces available."

"How to ensure each employee has a place to park."

Exercise: Can We Close Faster?

The Apparent Issue

You recently have been hired by Chaos, Inc., whose executives selected you to make immediate changes in how management accounting is done. You determine that their biggest challenge is the lack of timely feedback. The first issue you choose to address is the month-end closing process. Your goal is to reduce it from the current 12 days to 6. You interview the assistant controller, who tells you:

"Each month it takes long hours and the entire management accounting team's attention to close the general ledger. The process seems to go on forever, yet it has been like this for the past five years. It feels like we do not have enough people to make things easier because everyone is working long, hard days. We also have to delay all of our other work until the GL is closed and the reports are issued. By the end this process, everyone feels exhausted. It takes us a few days to recover, then we get back to our regular work. Two weeks later, it is crunch time again."

What would you define as the problem?

- How to...

- How to...

What would be another way to state the problem—via technology?

- How to...

- How to...

What would be another way to state the problem—via time?

- How to...

- How to...

What would be another way to state the problem—via the closing process?

- How to...

- How to...

What would be another way to state the problem—via the people involved?

- How to...

- How to...

CFO Lesson

The way you define a problem determines your solutions. Therefore, if you define the problem only one way, you limit your solutions, which may not be the ones that solve the problem to ensure that the fire goes out. Using a tool like problem restatement enables you to find the cause of the fire and create the optimal solution.

In the End

When your only tool is a hammer, all your problems look like nails.

The real issues or root cause of someone's lingering problem are often hidden behind a veil of smoke. As a solution creator or change agent, your task is to ignore the smoke and seek the cause. Furthermore, how you define the problem determines the solutions that you select.

By using probing questions and problem restatement, you will not view all your problems as nails. Instead, you will enable yourself to become a gifted problem solver, one who is valued by everyone with whom you work.

7

STEP 6½: IMPROVE BY MAKING A COMMITMENT

A dream can become real only after you make an emotional commitment to the dream

If you want to be promoted or take on more influential responsibilities, you must make a commitment to apply what you have learned. If you are still unconvinced that you need to improve what you do and how you do it, this final step may very well persuade you that the world of accounting is changing dramatically.

After reading this chapter, you should be able to

- take the last step toward improving your role.

- explain to your team how the world of accounting is changing.

- utilise other resources available to you.

- employ the Plus/Delta to document what works and what needs improvement.

GROWING PAINS

As you come to the end of this book, you may begin to feel overwhelmed by what is required to transform into a Key Financial Strategist. Please realise that many others have gone before you and have successfully made the transition to redefine their role. The best place to start is with a personal commitment to improve and grow. The pain of change that you may be feeling comes from your own ego, and is something that you must deal with and not ignore.

This chapter contains best practices for you to use in your commitment to grow out of your job. Just as the quote at the beginning of this chapter reminds us that there is a difference between a dream and a goal, keep in mind that your commitment is integral to this process.

Despite any trepidation that you may feel, remind yourself often that once you have made the transition to become a Key Financial Strategist, the rewards you receive will be tremendous and far outweigh the difficulties you may see ahead of you.

Exercise: Mistakes Made by Controllers and CFOs

Your friend Brian made many of these most common mistakes. At your next coaching session, as a way of reminding yourself that you are also fallible, you tell Brian about the mistakes you have made during your professional life.

I made the mistake of

_____ Not taking on the role that the company needs me to perform.

_____ Not recognising the power and influencing aspects of my role as the conscience of my organisation.

_____ Not creating a team approach, but instead trying to do it all by myself.

_____ Not becoming an equal participating member of my firm's leadership team.

_____ Not recognising the value and importance of corporate culture in making things happen.

_____ Not becoming a sales person for my team, my needs and my team's contributions.

_____ Not growing as an articulate communicator and tough negotiator.

_____ Not looking toward the future of my organisation and the changes in the management accounting profession.

_____ Not adding value to my firm in numerous, visible and measurable ways or touting these accomplishments to the executives.

_____ Not creating a network with other controllers or CFOs with whom I can share ideas and offer or get support.

Which of these have you made more than once?

Which of these have you learned from and changed your ways?

No. 3 Big Mistake of the CFO

Not addressing your workload killers

Another pitfall that the CFO should acknowledge is those areas that utilise a tremendous amount of your team's time and energy. By proactively planning for and addressing the following productivity sapping events, you will be able to keep your team and yourself on track.

- Mergers and acquisition activity
- Year-end closing
- Inventory taking and costing
- Peak sales season activity and transactions
- Sales promotion initiatives
- Budget development
- Annual planning process
- Employee education, including job cross-training
- Externally imposed deadlines for compliance purposes
- Personal time off
- Meetings infinitum

TODAY'S MANAGEMENT ACCOUNTING LEADER REALITIES

The following are five realities that you must face in order to make yourself and your team more effective. The "we" in these realities refers to you and your team as well as the management accounting profession.

1. Unless we change our thinking, tomorrow looks just like today.

2. Without a clear vision of tomorrow, what we expect tomorrow will not change from today.

3. If we raise our expectations, we alter our future vision.

4. Our skills and knowledge grow obsolete at an ever-faster rate.

5. A management accounting team advances in only two ways: (*a*) the solutions we provide and (*b*) the connections we sustain.

Our Skills and Knowledge Grow Obsolete at an Ever-Faster Rate

You must devote the necessary time and resources to training and educating your staff. The skills you and your team acquired as recently as three years ago are now outdated. Even if your employer does not provide you with funds for training, you must find ways to ensure your people are trained.

A Management Accounting Team Advances in Only Two Ways: The Solutions We Provide and the Connections We Sustain

Management accountants may be very good at finding solutions and very poor at maintaining connections. This is an area on which you must focus much of your attention. These connections include

- stepping outside your office and meeting with people, face-to-face, on a regular basis;
- making allies with your peers on the executive or management team; and
- becoming part of a networking group.

Solution 1—Get Out of Your Office

As a CFO or controller, you should spend 25% to 35% of your time meeting with those you serve, including major customers, investors, creditors and, of course, your peer managers.

Solution 2—Let Employees Out of the Department

Your employees should spend 10% to 15% of their time outside the management accounting department meeting with those they serve, for example, vendors, customers, bankers, service providers, coworkers and peers.

Solution 3—Create a "Stop Doing" List

In *Good to Great*,[1] Jim Collins offers good advice that will help your team get things done.

> Many of us lead busy but undisciplined lives. We have ever expanding "to do" lists, trying to build momentum by doing doing doing–and doing more. And it rarely works. Those who built good-to-great

companies, however, made as much use of "stop doing" lists as "to do" lists. They displayed a remarkable discipline to unplug all sorts of extraneous junk.

We spend so much time working on "what is due next" in management accounting that we rarely make an effort to discern what we should stop doing.

Accounting's Stop Doing List

- Titles and specialties

- Paper pushing

- Report issuing

- Analysis and spreadsheets

- Hand holding customers who make the same mistakes repeatedly

- Relying on faulty processes

- Interim GL closings

- One-off reports or analysis

- Treating errors as isolated events

SIGNIFICANT TRENDS IN MANAGEMENT ACCOUNTING THAT IMPACT THE CFO AND CONTROLLER

Trend No. 1

Exercise: The Cost of Processing Transactions Is Approaching Zero

Characterised by

FINANCE PROCESS	COST IN THE AVERAGE COMPANY	COST IN THE WORST COMPANY	COST IN THE WORLD CLASS COMPANY
A/R remittance processing	$0.67	$13.68	$0.01
P/R check processing	$1.91	$10.93	$0.36
A/P invoice processing	$2.93	$6.80	$0.35
Tracking fixed assets	$4.05	$19.10	$0.16
Expense report processing	$6.05	$25.75	$0.27
	Labour cost per transaction		

Source: *AICPA and the Hackett Group*

Trend No. 2

Everyone Demands Instant Gratification

This is characterised by

- the Internet.
- staying connected to the office 24/7.
- rise in use and popularity of social media.
- instant downloads of all media.
- wide-spread usage of G3 and G4 smart phones.
- satellite radio.
- executives who can get information on demand anywhere anytime, yet have to wait 10 days for the management accounting team to issue reports.

Trend No. 3

The Management Accounting Group Will Spend Less Time Processing and More Time Consulting

This is characterised by

- decentralisation of controls and management reporting.
- demand for real-time financial results.
- world-class companies are able to close within one day.
- finance must track, measure and report on nonfinancial data.
- time spent processing transactions must be reduced below 35% from its current 77%.

Trend No. 4

The Management Accounting Group Will Be Ever Smaller and Less Permanent

Examples from U.S. organisations are characterised by the following:

- The average finance group is between 33% to 70% smaller than it was 30 years ago for a company of the same size.
- The typical manager's span of control is approaching 75 employees, up from 5 employees in the 1970s.
- For every U.S. worker who loses his or her job, there are 25 employees who would leave their jobs if they could afford to do so.
- CEOs will continue use downsizing or rightsizing as a permanent management tool.

Trend No. 5

A Finance Professional's Employment Will Not Be Full-Time or "Permanent"

Examples from U.S. organisations are characterised by the following:

- Today's college graduate will have 5–8 different careers and spend 20% of his or her time unemployed before retiring.

- U.S. companies are relying on "just-in-time" employees to meet any growth in employment.

- Contingent workers make up between 25% to 33% of the U.S. workforce, and some experts predict that this number will grow to 50% in certain industries. (Contingent workers are part-time employees, contractors and leased employees.)

- 91% of businesses use temporary employees, which has resulted in the temporary industry growing tenfold over the past decade.

- 30% of all new jobs created are part-time and lower pay scale positions.

- American businesses are outsourcing finance and administrative work in record numbers.

Trend No. 6

Movement Toward a Pay-for-Performance Compensation System

Examples from U.S. organisations are characterised by

- wage increases to professionals that barely keep up with inflation.

- employers demanding that employees provide positive proof that they are earning their compensation.

- profit-sharing plans and stock options are replacing annual raises.

- dramatic growth in self-directed pension accounts and disfavour towards defined benefit accounts.

- a "what have you done for me lately" mentality widespread amongst executives and managers.

Trend No. 7

Management Accountants Required to Have a Base of Knowledge Broader Than Accounting or Finance

Examples from U.S. organisations are characterised by the following:

- Almost all management accounting is done using technology that did not exist 10 years ago.

- The profession requires a five-year degree in order to become a CPA.

- During a merger the employees retained are those who have skills beyond accounting.

- Continued outsourcing of low-value work like A/P and tax preparation.

- By the year 2020, more than 50% of all American workers will need some retraining because their skills have become obsolete.

- A novel technology's life cycle is less than 18 months.

- The next generation of workers knows more about technology and social media than the people they work for.

Trend No. 8

Reliance on Task Forces and Project Teams

This trend is characterised by the following changes:

- Work is perceived as a series of projects staffed by employees whose expertise is required to bring them to fruition.

- Due to poor communication, management more heavily relies on cross-functional task forces and project teams to accomplish work.

- CEOs and the human resources team seek out management accountants who can work well with others.

- More employees fall into the just-in-time category.

- The ever higher cost of travel prevents employees who work together from meeting face-to-face.

- Increasing numbers of organisations have locations spread across the globe.

- Global businesses operate in multiple time zones simultaneously.

Trend No. 9

Increase in Need for Compliance and Governance That Does Not Waste Resources

This trend is characterised by

- regulatory compliance and complexity.

- current and past scandals regarding financial reporting, stock options and pro forma earnings.

- more and more reliance on technology instead of people to make decisions and process transactions, leading to lack of awareness of work quality.

Answer These Questions

How will these trends affect your company in the future? How are they affecting it now?

How will these trends affect you and your team?

How will these trends affect your career?

Do you see other management accounting trends?

Which trend will have the biggest impact on you? Why?

How can you best start preparing today for tomorrow?

STRATEGIES FOR COPING WITH THE PAIN OF THESE CHANGES

- *Strategy No. 1*—Climb on board, support these changes and learn from them.
- *Strategy No. 2*—Treat your employees like volunteers, especially with respect and dignity.
- *Strategy No. 3*—Go out and get practical experiences outside management accounting.
- *Strategy No. 4*—Commit to lifelong learning.
- *Strategy No. 5*—Take your skills seriously, but not your title or position.
- *Strategy No. 6*—Remind yourself often that you are replaceable.

BEST PRACTICE—INSTILLING A PERSONAL COMMITMENT

Formalising actionable goals is an important best practice to consider. Figure 7-1 outlines a simple, but effective leadership action plan commitment document.

Figure 7-1: Your Commitment to a Leadership Action Plan

I commit to taking these actions, and I will check back with myself to verify that I have done something on or around _____ (follow-up date).

Date prepared _____

My signature _____

My accountability partner is _____

I will check in with my accountability partner every _____ days.

Exercise: What Is Your Next Step?

Now that you have plenty of information about how to add value to your organisation while boosting your career, it is time to determine your next steps. Complete your own action plan below.

How do you envision your role as controller or CFO six months from now?

What are you willing to do to improve your role as a shaper of your team's and organisation's corporate culture?

What will be the long-term payoff of the changes you will implement?

What specific resources will you need in the future?

- Coach _____

- Mentor _____

- Specific training _____

- More support _____

BEST PRACTICE—INSTILLING CONTINUOUS IMPROVEMENT WITH PLUS/DELTA

The Plus/Delta Analysis is an excellent learning tool for every meeting, project or performance evaluation (see figure 7-2).

The Plus/Delta Analysis is a summary of what is worth repeating and what needs improving. It spawns rapid improvements, shortens learning curves and increases accountability.

Figure 7-2: The Plus/Delta Tool

PLUSES +	DELTAS Δ
(THINGS THAT WORK AND SHOULD BE KEPT)	(THINGS THAT SHOULD CHANGE OR BE BETTER)

Steps of the Plus/Delta

1. Announce to everyone involved with the improvement effort the purpose of the Plus/Delta.

2. Spend time gathering a list of things that worked well and list them on the "Plus" side. Keep building this list until it is complete or there are no more suggestions.

3. Spend time gathering a list of things that people would like to see changed and list them on the "Delta" side. Keep building this list until it is complete or there are no more suggestions.

4. Before the next session or meeting, address the changes that were recommended and accommodate those that cannot be changed.

5. Start the next meeting by reviewing the most recent Plus/Delta.

6. Remind everyone that you will continue to pursue items from the Plus list that are working well.

7. Inform the team of the changes that will come from the Delta list.

8. Explain which changes cannot be implemented, then brainstorm alternatives.

9. Continue to use the Plus/Delta tool at each meeting, event or gathering.

10. Notice and celebrate how improvements quickly take place.

This is good documentation to retain for demonstrating to others that you are being proactive in addressing employee suggestions for improvement and are listening to your best resources. Even better, it models for others what it takes to be an agent of change.

Endnotes

1 Collins, Jim. *Good to Great*. HarperBusiness. 2001.

CONTROLLER'S RESOURCES LIST

Following are resources to help you add value as a CFO or controller, especially when coaching organisations or teams.

Performance Scorecards: Measuring the Right Things in the Real World
Richard Y. Chang and Mark W. Morgan, Jossey-Bass

The HR Scorecard
Brian Becker, Mark Huselid, Dave Ulrich, Harvard Business School

Balanced Scorecard Step by Step: Maximizing Performance & Maintaining Results
Paul R. Niven, John Wiley & Sons

The Balanced Scorecard: Translating Strategy into Action
Robert S. Kaplan and David P. Norton, Harvard Business School

Built to Last: Successful Habits of Successful Companies
J.C. Collins and J. I. Porras, Harper Collins

The 80/20 Principle: the Secret of Achieving More with Less
Richard Koch, Doubleday Dell Publishing

High Performance Benchmarking: 20 Steps to Success
H. James Harrington and James S. Harrington, McGraw Hill

Keeping Score: Using the Right Metrics to Drive World-Class Performance
Mark Graham Brown, Quality Resources

The Profit Zone: How Strategic Business Decisions Will Lead You to Tomorrow's Profits
Adrian Slywotzky and David Morrison, Three Rivers Press

Profit Patterns: 30 Ways to Anticipate and Profit from Strategic Forces Reshaping Your Business
Adrian Slywotzky and David Morrison, Times Business Press

Women Lead the Way
Linda Tarr-Whelan, Berrett-Koehler Publishers

See Jane Lead
Lois P. Frankel, Business Plus

Printed in the United States
By Bookmasters